Maine Coon Cats

The Owners Guide from Kitten to Old Age

Buying, Caring for, Grooming, Health, Training, and
Understanding Your Maine Coon

By Rosemary Kendall

Copyright and Trademarks

Disclaimer and Legal Notice

Foreword

Like most people, my initial attraction to the Maine Coon breed was their wonderful size. I love big cats, and a really large Maine Coon can get upward of 25 lbs. / 11.34 kg. That's pretty much the ideal cat in my book.

The first Maine Coon I met, however, was the runt of the litter and no larger than any other domestic cat. I was housesitting for friends in, of all places, Maine. My friend apologized for Lucy, saying, "She didn't get the Maine Coon handbook on personality either. She's kinda shy."

These cats are known for natures so gregarious and affable they're almost dog-like in their interactions; following their people from room to room and preferring to lie nearby companionably rather than feeling a dire need to be in the middle of everything.

I was to be there for almost a month, so Lucy and I had time. Not knowing quite what else to do, I just started talking. At first I would only get glimpses of her, but I kept up my end of the conversation. By Friday of the first week, the strikingly beautiful orange and white cat, known as a "red" in this breed, was sitting in the door of the hallway watching TV with me. Sunday night she joined me in bed, and Monday morning we read the newspaper together.

Something I said, I'll never know what, sealed the deal between us and for the rest of the month, I had a shadow around the house. Often in the evenings Lucy curled up on the couch while I read, and invariably she trotted down the hall with me at bedtime.

The trademark Maine Coon humor surfaced, in fact, over my

reading glasses, which she loved to nudge out of place. I'm one of those reluctant eyeglass wearers. I take them off when they slide down on my face and set them aside in annoyance, only to reach for them in greater irritation because all books and newspapers are printed with such tiny type today.

Never one time when I was in that house with Lucy could I find my glasses where I sat them down. They weren't harmed in any way. They weren't hidden exactly, but they weren't where I left them, and I swear that cat was grinning at me.

I discovered she was happily adept at games of paper wad soccer, and would even fetch a little. By the time my friends returned, Lucy and I had bonded solidly and she was always glad to see me when I came for other visits in the future.

It wasn't long after that, at a cat show, when I saw my first really big Maine Coon male, a red, like Lucy. Within a couple of months, I purchased a kitten from a breeder. I was hooked and within five years I was running my own cattery. This was a most unexpected development in my life, becoming a vocation and avocation that has consumed me for many years.

I've raised several cat breeds through the years, including Maine Coons. Of all the breeds with which I've worked, I've found them to be the most consistently social. Yes, a Siamese will dog your every step and demand to know your schedule in triplicate, commenting loudly all the time.

A Maine Coon is just that devoted, but tons less, well . . . potentially neurotic. (Apologies to all Siamese lovers, but don't get one until you have the time and capacity to commit to the relationship!)

Maine Coons are interested and curious by nature. They want to be with you. They'll make you laugh, and they will manage your life — sweetly, with melodic trilling chirps that are so adorable coming out of cats that big, you'll be entranced all over again.

Yes, they are longhaired cats, but trust me. I've lived with Persians. With regular combing and brushing, and the occasional trip into see the groomer, the silky and weather resilient coat of the Maine Coon is very manageable. These are, however, indoor cats, as all domestic breeds should be.

(Very large Maine Coons are at particular danger for being mistaken for wild animals and there are a lot of idiots in the world.)

I hope to give you an introduction to the Maine Coon and to their basic care, as well as some insight into life with cats in general.

There really aren't enough good things I can say about this breed, and I think when you meet them, both in the pages of this book and in person, you'll feel the same way.

Photo Credit: Kat Doring of Kats Kits

Acknowledgments

In writing this book, I also sought tips, advice, photos, and opinions from many experts of the Maine Coon breed.

In particular I wish to thank the following wonderful experts for going out of their way to help and contribute:

Sharon Stegall of Dracoonfly Maine Coon Cattery
http://www.dracoonfly.com

Terrie Lyons of Budletts Maine Coons
http://www.mainecoonkittens.me.uk

Robin Warren of Red Flannel Cattery
http://redflannelcattery.com/

Mary Turcotte of Cameronwoods Maine Coons
http://www.cameronwoodsmainecoons.com

Johnnie Hardee of Megacoon Cattery
http://www.megacoon.com

Mareen Holden-Ritchie of Amoramist Maine Coons
http://www.amoramist.com

Kat Doring of Kats Kits
http://www.katskits.com

Brooke Hughes of Rock Hill Maine Coons
http://www.rockhillmainecoons.com/

Table of Contents

Table of Contents

Chapter 1 - The World of the Maine Coon

The primary reason people give for being interested in the Maine Coon is the size of the breed. Big, burly males can average 15-25 lbs. / 6.8-11.3 kg. Females are smaller, but still pleasantly solid at 10-15 lbs. / 4.53-6.8 kg.

Individuals of either gender may grow to even greater sizes. And it's not just weight. Stewie, a Maine Coon that died of cancer in 2013, held the Guinness Record as the world's longest domestic cat at 48.5 inches / 123.19 cm from the tip of his nose to the end of his tail. That's more than four feet or 1.23 meters!

The Maine Coon is, in fact, the largest of all the domestic cats and America's native longhaired breed. But the real draw, in my opinion, is the Maine Coon's superior, highly companionable personality. Although very people-oriented, these cats aren't needy or dependent. They like to hang out with their humans in an easygoing, laid back kind of way.

If you want to have a big (and at times, even goofy) sidekick with fur, you'll be hard pressed to find a better cat than a Maine Coon. He'll be your constant wingman. Affectionate, amusing, and family oriented, this is one of the most liked of all pedigreed cat breeds for the simple reason that they're loyal and steadfast chums for their people.

Maine Coons Should Be Indoor Pets

I do want to say from the beginning that I never allow any of my cats, regardless of breed, to go outside. All of my cats are indoor pets and I strongly recommend taking this attitude with your own pets.

Many Maine Coons are large enough and "wild" looking enough to be mistaken for wildlife. There are a lot of idiotic people with guns in this world. "Outside" isn't safe for our pets in my opinion anyway, but I want to doubly emphasize this point for Maine Coons.

It doesn't matter how hardy they are by constitution, or how weather resistant their coat is by nature's gift. Maine Coons should be indoor cats.

What is a "Registered" Pedigree?

Before I introduce you to the Maine Coon in detail, let's look at exactly what it means to adopt a cat that has a registered pedigree. To be 100% certain that you are indeed adopting a purebred Maine Coon, you must locate a cattery that specializes in the breed, and purchase a kitten with a traceable "family tree."

As proof of the legitimacy of their bloodlines, catteries associate themselves with one or more of the major cat registries. By doing this, they assure potential customers of the authenticity of their breed claims.

Although there are several cat registries, the largest and best known are the Cat Fanciers' Association (CFA) and The International Cat Association (TICA). A cat has to be registered with either group, for instance, to be shown in an exhibition sponsored by that entity.

Kittens born in catteries are classed as either "show quality" or "pet quality." The latter are the kittens that are made available to average potential buyers desirous of acquiring a family cat.

Clearly this is not the only venue for adopting a Maine Coon cat, but by working with a cattery where the animals have registered pedigrees, you will be seeing the finest examples of the breed you can find.

You will also have the benefit of adopting a kitten produced from verifiable bloodlines that are actively cultivated to avoid potential genetic health problems.

(I'll discuss more on this topic in the chapter on health, but the two primary conditions associated with the breed are hip dysplasia and hypertrophic cardiomyopathy.)

Brief History of the Maine Coon Breed

Although it's a ridiculous notion that the Maine Coon is a cross between a domestic cat and a raccoon, this is still a story that gets circulated. Not only is it not true, it's genetically impossible!

There is a charming "origin" legend, however, about a cabin boy on an ocean-going vessel. He collected beautiful longhaired cats to bring good fortune to his ship and to control rats onboard.

The boy's name was Tom Coon and the story says he continued to collect "Maine cats" after he became a sea captain. When Coon went ashore, his cats went with him, where they — like any lusty sailor on shore leave — intermingled with the local cats until, in time, a distinct line of "Maine Coon" cats evolved.

Without question, these heavily boned and thickly furred cats became well adapted to life in the harsh Maine winters and were useful on local farms to control vermin. Their long, sturdy legs helped them to get through, over, or around all sorts of obstacles — from deep snow to rocky ground — and they won a reputation as premier barn cats.

Certainly the breed has been well established for more than a century, but one line of thinking suggests its genetics are actually linked to Norwegian Forest Cats brought to North American by the Vikings sometime around the year 1000.

It's even possible the Maine Coon can claim a relationship to Marie Antoinette's beloved cats. Unlike the royal family, the six white Turkish Angoras escaped the French Revolution with the aid of Captain Samuel Clough. The former royal pets finished out their lives in Wiscasset, Maine, where, in all likelihood, they interbred with local cats.

Although the complete puzzle of the Maine Coon's evolution may never be sorted out, it is now Maine's official state cat. Once considered a working cat and a mouser, Maine Coons are now beloved and pampered house pets. They have exceptional personalities, are highly intelligent, and by nature are agreeable and trainable.

Physical Characteristics and Personality

The Maine Coon is characterized as a "medium to large" cat. Some females can be as small as 10 lbs. / 4.53 kg, with big males often going up to 25 lbs. / 11.3 kg. A fair average is around 18 lbs. / 8.16 kg. But frankly, even an "average" Maine Coon looks bigger.

Mareen Holden-Ritchie of Amoramist Maine Coons told me that she had a Maine Coon who went to his pet home when he retired, and his weight was 36 pounds!

With broad chests, rectangular bodies, solid musculature, and a big-boned frame, everything about a Maine Coon connotes size and substance. Add to the picture big ears and big tufted feet, and you have the perfect image of a gentle feline giant. They have a lifespan of 12-15 years.

The somewhat shaggy coat of the Maine Coon is shorter over the shoulders and down the front legs, but begins to lengthen along the back and sides. The neck fur may, however, form a thick mane, not unlike a lion's. The cat's britches are especially long and full, as is the belly fur.

A flowing, bushy tail roughly the same length as the body caps off the overall luxurious "look." The tail is often ringed, which has given more currency to the silly myth about the cat being a feline / raccoon hybrid.

It's almost impossible *not* to want to pet a Maine Coon when you see one. When you touch the cat, you'll find his water resistant and insulating coat to be both silky and soft, with a glossy sheen. There are tufts of fur between the paw pads, as well as luxuriant tufts growing out of the ears, which may also have lynx tips.

The ear tufting and decidedly prominent cheekbones give the Maine Coon a vaguely "wild" appearance, but the green to gold eyes give him away. Set wide in a box-like face, they gaze outward with benign patience, clearly showing the Maine Coon to be fully domesticated to the point of complacency.

For his solid bulk and size, however, the Maine Coon's voice is a gentle chirping trill. He's a soft-voiced fellow and his comments are delivered with something approaching ironic humor. They're talkers and commentators.

It's easy to believe these cats go about laughing at the absurdities of life, an impression the breed bolsters with a reputation for downright silly antics. The kittenish behavior never goes away; it's there for life with a Maine Coon.

They grow slowly, taking 3-4 years to reach full maturity. During that time their loving and sweet dispositions seem to mellow into affectionate adulthood.

They exhibit great loyalty to their humans and are social cats, following their people from room to room and providing "assistance" and "supervision" for the current project at hand. They don't just like human companionship; they actively seek it out.

A Family Cat?

The Maine Coon makes a really fantastic family cat. They aren't lap cats per se, but they do want to be a part of whatever's going on around the house in a supervisory capacity.

They not only get along well with children, but they do perfectly fine with other pets, including dogs. Maine Coons are no more difficult to acclimate in multi-cat households than any other breed. In fact, Maine Coons are so easy-going, that in spite of their size, they may be the ones to be picked on in a feline territorial dispute.

Don't worry that he'll use his size to his advantage. I did have a Maine Coon once that would get a rowdy younger cat to calm down by lying on him, but that's about as much "aggression" as he ever managed.

If a Maine Coon doesn't like what's going on, he simply manages to be somewhere else. That being said, I am a firm believer that all children must be taught to deal respectfully and gently with animals. You shouldn't rely on the cat to be the "responsible adult" in the situation.

Any cat, regardless of breed and no matter how well-behaved, will react badly if it is being harassed or handled roughly. In those situations, I frankly think it is the child that needs to be instructed in better behavior, not the cat.

And, while we are speaking of cats being cats, I wouldn't really trust any breed with the family parakeet or aquarium fish. In multi-species households, careful segregation should be the order of the day. Tightly-latched cages and secure aquarium lids make for good neighbors.

Multiple Maine Coons?

Multiple numbers of Maine Coons will get along quite well in a household and two cats acquired at the same time, or adopted from the same litter, will do especially well together. You will be responsible for the regular combing of two cats, but the Maine Coon is so much more low maintenance in this regard than other longhaired breeds that this really isn't a daunting chore.

Male or Female?

This is a standard question, and one I'm frankly not sure has any validity with this breed. I really do not see a lot of difference in the personality and temperament of the genders. All Maine Coon cats are calm, even-tempered, affectionate, and even comical cats.

They are a joy, pure and simple.

Selecting the gender of your pet is purely a matter of personal preference. Spraying is rarely, if ever, an issue with neutered males and, as you will learn, neutering is a condition of pet quality adoptions. So even this consideration (which is blown completely out of proportion in my opinion) is not a basis for choosing a male over a female.

"Types" of Maine Coon Cats

It is a mistake to assume that there is more than one "type" of Maine Coon, but they do come in every color and pattern, except lavender, chocolate, or pointed like a "Siamese." All told, there are more than 60 possible color combinations. For all coat types the eye color ranges across shades of green and gold, but in white cats it is possible to see blue or odd eyes (one blue eye, the other gold.)

The solid coat colors include white, black, cream, blue (Maltese), and red. The breed standard calls for the shades to be uniform, with no variations or a suggestion of tabby markings. Black Maine Coons should not have any hint of "rust." A "smoke" Maine Coon has a solid coat with a lighter undercoat that seems almost "faded."

You will see bi-colors like the popular black and white "tuxedo" cats, as well as parti-colors, known commonly as calicos. Tortoiseshell or "tortie" Maine Coons have a black base color with patches of cream and red, while a "tortie" has color stripes instead of patches.

The tabby-coat is perhaps the best known of all the Maine Coon markings and can be present in all colors, with red being a particular favorite. Tabby means the kitten has stripes, like tiger stripes. There are two variations: mackerel and classic. Both have the famous M on the forehead. A mackerel tabby has stripes running down the body with a connecting stripe down the back, like a zebra (see below).

Photo Credits: Robin Warren of Red Flannel Cattery

The classic tabby has wide stripes on the legs, face, and tail, but the stripes on the body are random and swirled with a bulls-eye on the belly (see previous page).

Grooming Requirements

Although a longhaired breed, the Maine Coon does not need the kind of constant grooming required by other heavily coated cats, like the Persian. Perhaps because the Maine Coon does have "forest cat" blood, their silky fur resists tangling and can be well managed with regular combing. They do have some tendency to have oily fur, however, and benefit from periodic baths, including degreasing.

I'll discuss this more fully in the chapter on daily care, but oddly enough, Maine Coons do not necessarily shed more than any other breed of cat. They will experience periods of seasonal shedding as the warm months are coming on, but for all their luxuriant appearance, the degree to which they shed is much more an individual characteristic than an overall breed trait.

Similar Breeds

The Norwegian Forest Cat is often confused with the Maine Coon. "Weegies" are also big cats, averaging 14-16 lbs. / 6.35-7.25 kg., and like the Maine Coon, are slow to mature, not reaching their full size until at least six years of age. They are hardy and long-lived cats, often reaching 14-16 years.

The Weegie is also a strikingly beautiful cat with large, almond-shape eyes set more obliquely in its face than those of the Maine Coon. Overall, a Weegie's face is more triangular, rather than square and solid like a Maine Coon's.

You can, in fact, trace a perfect equilateral triangle from the point of a Weegie's nose to the base of his ears and across the forehead. Both breeds do have luxuriantly "furnished" ears and handsome flowing whiskers.

The Norwegian Forest Cat, however, is a superior climber with strong and sturdy claws. The Maine Coon usually prefers to keep his paws solidly on the ground. He'll chase things down at ground level, but you won't often catch him headed to the top of the curtains like a Weegie.

Still, if you prefer a slightly smaller, but solidly built and muscular cat with a "wild" appearance and long hair, the Norwegian Forest Cat fits the bill perfectly. They have an overall appearance that is both rugged and refined, and they are sweet and good-natured companions.

Maine Coon Pros and Cons

I have never been all that comfortable with putting together a list of pros and cons for any type of animal, much less for any specific breed within the species. Here's why:

I love dogs. I was raised with Yorkshire Terriers and love their feisty dispositions and determined way of being in the world, but I have absolutely no desire to own a dog for the simple reason that I don't want to have to walk one. Another person might say that is the *best* reason to have a dog. My "con" is their "pro."

For me, changing a litter box is just a mindless chore, not pleasant or unpleasant, just something that has to be done. Other people think it's the worst job imaginable. Those folks don't need to be keeping a cat of any breed.

I think Maine Coons are great cats — funny, lovable, and best of all, seriously big! I love their massive bodies and the satisfying weight of the *thunk* they make landing on the bed, even if they do stair-step their way up from the floor rather than jump.

There's just something wonderfully regular and steady about a Maine Coon, almost unflappable. They're not loud voiced or given to protests like a Siamese. They're not neurotic or plagued with separation anxiety. A Maine Coon just deals with what's going on in the moment.

In addition to their size, they have few genetic issues. Having dealt with serious health issues in other breeds, the hardiness of the Maine Coon is, for me, a big "selling" point. It's also nice to be able to enjoy the luxuriant feel of a longhaired breed without the constant grooming needs of a cat, like the Persian.

So you see, from the perspective of a life-long cat lover, I just don't see a lot of "cons" to owning a Maine Coon. They're fantastic cats and probably in my top five favorite breeds.

I have to confess that my favorite cat is the "plain" Domestic Shorthair or "alley" cat, for the simple reason that he's an honest working fellow who doesn't come with a high learning curve.

Of all the pedigreed cats, however, I'd say the same for the Maine Coon. Some writers even characterize them as the perfect "beginner's cat."

A Word on Rescue Adoptions

I think it's always important in any book on cats or dogs to put in a good word for the superior work being done by volunteers in rescue shelters around the world.

If you have your heart set on adopting a Maine Coon, I'm certainly not going to discourage you, but if you simply want a loving pet, you can pair your desire for a cat with the benevolent act of saving a life.

There are thousands of lovely cats in foster care that need "forever" homes. The people and groups that work with these animals are, in my estimation, real "angels." From unwanted kittens to abandoned senior cats, the supply of needy animals is never ending.

Please don't rule out one of these worthy cats as you consider becoming a "cat person," and please support the efforts of rescue groups regardless. These entities are always strapped for cash, and they are doing wonderful and compassionate work.

Chapter 2 - Finding a Maine Coon Breeder

Any time you are considering adopting a pedigreed cat like a Maine Coon, you have to ask yourself why you want an animal with "papers." A cat with a pedigree isn't really any different than other cat; he can just produce his family tree, going back 4-5 generations.

Pedigreed cats can be registered with cat associations because they are qualified examples of their type and they will "breed true." This simply means if you mate a Maine Coon male with a Maine Coon female, the kittens will have the same physical traits as the parents.

But since most people cannot afford show quality animals, and pet quality adoptions require spaying and neutering, breeding is rarely a basis for getting a pedigreed cat.

Breeders work toward achieving the points of the recognized "breed standard" for the cats they raise. This is the accepted list of requirements to achieve perfection in any breed group, which is in turn used as the basis for judging animals that compete in organized cat shows.

Therefore, the best and only reason to adopt a pedigreed cat, in my opinion, is love of the breed. Pedigreed cats aren't fashion accessories and shouldn't be adopted on a whim. You should know the breed, and value it for its specific and special qualities.

In doing so, and in working with qualified and reputable breeders, you are supporting the continued cultivation of the cats according to the accepted standard of excellence, rather than supporting the activities of "kitten mills."

I would never suggest that a "backyard breeder," someone who owns a Maine Coon and has allowed that animal to have kittens, does not care about their welfare. I'm talking about breeders who churn out as many kittens as they can, with no thought to the health of the mother or her offspring, because they have nothing in mind but profit.

The best catteries are full-time, breed-specific operations completely dedicated to the cultivation and welfare of the cats. This is the type of breeder you want to support and with whom you want to do business.

Pet Quality vs. Show Quality

Adopting a purebred cat is an expensive proposition at best. Since most people only want a beautiful companion animal of a specific type, they will be looking at "pet-quality" kittens from a recognized cattery.

Pet-quality kittens are not "sub-standard." They simply don't conform precisely enough to the recognized breed standard to be shown in exhibition or to be used in breeding programs.

For people outside the cat "fancy," the reasons for this designation will probably be too esoteric to even be detected. Certainly the "flaw" won't be consequential enough to be an adoption "deal breaker." Pet-quality kittens are beautiful animals with excellent pedigrees.

The one caveat of a pet-quality adoption is that the animals must be spayed or neutered. This requirement is specifically to protect the purity of the cattery's bloodlines and to prevent undesirable traits from being passed on.

Understanding How Catteries Operate

The process of adopting a pedigreed cat may be protracted. People who have never worked with a cattery may not understand that it's not as simple as driving up and announcing, "I want to buy a kitten." While you will certainly be stating your intention to do so, you'd be far better off to treat the matter as an adoption, not a transaction.

Breeders dedicate a major portion of their lives to caring for their cats and to selectively honing their cattery's bloodlines to create premier representatives of the breed. They *care* about their cats and they don't have to sell one to you. Your suitability as a parent for their babies is fair game for scrutiny, as it should be when the welfare of a living creature is at stake.

Frankly, I wouldn't work with a breeder who shows one ounce less commitment. If you see an advertisement for a "cattery" that even suggests you can just walk in with cash and walk out with a cat, you are likely dealing with a kitten mill. No true cat lover wants to support that kind of operation.

I, myself, have declined to allow certain interested parties to adopt one of my kittens because I wasn't comfortable that the baby would be going to a loving and attentive home. If I can't confirm that one of my cats will have their physical and emotional needs met, then there's not enough money in the world to "seal the deal."

My best advice to you is to regard the adoption of a pedigreed cat as a two-way exchange. I expect to answer specific questions and to ask them. Hopefully, I am both clear and polite about why I'm doing this. I do tell prospective clients that I'm not trying to give them the third-degree, but that I must have assurances about the safety and care of the cat.

Over the years there have been a couple of times when someone has been offended and refused to have this conversation with me. Those people didn't go home with one of my cats.

Now, for my part in the exchange, I maintain a complete list of both former clients and colleagues that I am happy to provide as references. Every person on the list is willing to discuss working with me and living with my cats. A breeder who will not provide references to you would, in my opinion, not be someone you'd want to deal with.

Finding and Evaluating Reputable Breeders

When I became interested in the Maine Coon breed, I was already a bona fide "crazy cat lady" with years of experience in the cat fancy. I knew what steps to take to locate a breeder and how to negotiate an adoption. Thankfully, this is a highly popular breed, so you shouldn't have any difficulty finding a good cattery.

Attend Cat Shows

To really start to familiarize yourself with the breed, however, and to make contact with professional breeders in your area, I'd recommend attending cat shows.

I'll discuss these venues more fully later in the book, but for now, let's just address the fact that at a cat show you can see beautiful examples of the breed and collect business cards from catteries.

Don't expect to get a breeder's undivided attention at a show, however, or to open negotiations for an adoption. Cat shows are unbelievably hectic and they aren't intended to be the site of business activity, anyway.

Essentially, you'll be window-shopping. It's perfectly acceptable to ask questions and to say, "May I have your business card? I'd like to contact you to talk about your cats." I wouldn't bluntly blurt out, "I want to buy one of your cats." That's presumptuous and sets the wrong opening tone.

You can inquire about current availability and the proposed breeding schedule for the year. Well-organized catteries carefully schedule litters and can give you a reasonably accurate idea of when you might be able to adopt.

You will pose your real in-depth questions in a lengthier telephone conversation and when you visit the cattery in person, which you should always do, perhaps more than once, before you adopt a kitten.

Information You Want From the Breeder

Be prepared for your first visit to a cattery. You'll forget how to speak English and will spend a lot of time cooing and saying,

"Awwwwwww!!!"

Even after years in the cat fancy, I find it hard to treat being surrounded by gorgeous cats and kittens as a business transaction. The excitement of contemplating having a new baby in the house, who will become your companion for years, never gets old.

Maine Coon kittens get me every time, especially when they have the lynx ear tips. Those wide, curious eyes and all that fluffy baby fur redefines adorable for me. Is it any wonder that breeders closely question prospective "parents" for those precious little creatures?

You should have all of your questions prepared in advance, including some of the following points.

- How long has the cattery been established?
- How big is the operation?
- Do they work with breeds other than the Maine Coon?

Now or in the past?
- Does the breeder exhibit the animals in organized cat shows? Why or why not?

Beware of dealing with any breeder who, when presented with these and similar questions:

- Is vague or evasive with their responses and seems to lack a basic knowledge of the breed.
- Denies that potential genetic issues are associated with the breed or assures you that all such problems have been completed eradicated from their cats.
- Doesn't seem to be actively involved with the cats.
- Refuses to let your tour the cattery or to interact with the cats.
- Can't produce documentation of health screenings and ancestry.
- Brushes off the need for all cats to be properly socialized before adoption.

Ask about both the kitten's parents.

- Are they healthy?
- How many litters has the female delivered?
- Have all of her kittens from past litters been healthy?
- Who is the father?
- Have the two cats produced litters together in the past?
- Why have these cats been chosen as a breeding pair?

You should be allowed to see the health records for both cats. Examine the information carefully. Make sure the cats have seen a veterinarian on a routine basis and have received their vaccinations.

If other tests and procedures are listed, find out why they were required. Make note of words or phrases you don't understand and either look them up online or discuss them with your own vet.

If possible, meet and interact with the parents. Their personalities are not necessarily a measurement of the kitten's nature, but I've found it to be a pretty good indicator, especially in a breed as sweet-natured as the Maine Coon.

- What kind of health care did the female receive during her pregnancy?
- How did the delivery go?
- Was it a normal birth?
- Were the kittens able to nurse without problems?
- Have they needed any special health care?
- Have they ever been treated for fleas or worms?
- Have they received their first vaccination?
- When are the boosters due?
- Will you receive copies of all the health records?

Always make certain that you understand any type of health guarantee that is included in the adoption agreement and what, if anything, you have to do — like have the baby evaluated by a veterinarian, to ensure the guarantee is not voided.

Genetic Health Conditions

Maine Coons are extremely hardy cats and they are not prone to a large number of illnesses. They can, however, develop both hip dysplasia and hypertrophic cardiomyopathy. In truth, though, these conditions can be present in cats of all breeds. Within a careful breeding program, incidences should be minimal.

Socialization Methods

It's especially important to discuss socialization with the breeder. Most kittens are not made available for adoption until they have reached 3 months of age. By then, they should be litter box trained and familiar with a scratching post, in addition to having been weaned.

Breeders who are conscientious about preparing kittens for adoption ensure that the babies are handled every day, interact with other cats of all ages, and have lots of opportunities to explore. All of this intellectual stimulation is essential to keep those bright, curious little minds happy. A bored kitten is trouble on four paws!

The kittens should also have reasonable exposure to normal household and environmental circumstances. Here's a good example of why this is so important. Ten years ago I adopted two cats from the same litter, in this instance Russian Blues, who had been in foster care for 11 months.

They were, and are, lovely cats, but they had never seen another human being. The woman who cared for them admitted she had no friends. After all this time with me, my boys still evaporate into their secret hiding places when people come into our home.

When cats are exposed to noises, other animals, children, and just life in general at a young age, they are less reactive and anxious as adults. Maine Coons have a reputation for being naturally well adjusted, but this does not eliminate the need for that early socialization.

Information the Breeder Wants From You

Again, the process of adopting a pedigreed cat like a Maine Coon should involve give and take. If you expect the breeder to answer your questions, you should be willing to answer some as well about yourself and your lifestyle. This is not a matter of prying on the part of the breeder, but is rather an attempt to make a good judgment on the animal's behalf.

By nature, the Maine Coon is not a needy cat, but they do love their people. They tend to get on well with other pets, and are easy enough in their disposition to be highly suitable "first time" cats. I always ask any potential "parent" if they have previous experience with cats, and if so, what kind.

In doing so, I want to have a basis for making comparisons about things like temperament and grooming needs. Someone who has, for instance, owned a Persian might expect to be tied to a complicated grooming regimen because the Maine Coon is also longhaired. In reality, however, these cats are infinitely easier to care for than other longhaired varieties.

Someone who has lived with a Siamese might expect loud and opinionated yowling when they learn that the Maine Coon also has a reputation as a talkative breed. A Siamese in full voice could raise the dead. A Maine Coon, on the other hand, chirps and trills melodically and is a joy to listen to no matter how much he has to say.

When I discuss this kind of thing with a prospective Maine Coon owner, I listen to how the person responds. I like people who ask lots of questions and are clearly trying to learn everything about the breed from the onset of the relationship.

Take my advice on this point. Do not try to game a breeder with false interest or overblown claims about your knowledge and intent to care for the cat. We want to see our kittens go to people who are as passionate about their welfare as we are.

My favorite question to ask is, "Where will the kitten sleep?" I know I have a real winner of a potential "parent" when the answer is prefaced with a blank stare followed by, "Why, with me, of course." I'm also fine with, "Anywhere he wants."

You might also be asked how much you travel, who will care for the cat while you are away, and if you have a veterinarian. Again, this isn't being nosey. I'm perfectly prepared to give clients living in my area a list of good pet sitters and outstanding veterinarians.

Most breeders, myself included, want to be an ongoing resource for their clients after the kitten leaves the cattery. I call to check up on my babies periodically, so it's important to me to have a friendly rapport with all my clients.

When I say this, the response and level of receptiveness I get from the person with whom I'm talking tells me a great deal. Sometimes, if the whole thing just doesn't feel right, I do say no to the adoption.

Chapter 3 - Finalizing the Adoption

At the point at which you actually get to meet and play with the Maine Coon kittens, be prepared to be asked to use hand sanitizer. This is a good sign that you are working with a knowledgeable breeder. The request is to protect the cats, not you. Many feline diseases are highly communicable. Stringent sanitation precautions are necessary.

The first time you hold a baby Maine Coon, you'll be absolutely floored by their sweetness and what soft, fluffy little fur balls they are. Still, you should be paying attention to some particulars about the kitten's condition — while you're cooing baby talk and picking out names.

- The coat should be lusciously soft and completely intact with no bald spots or matting. The kitten should smell and feel clean.

- Get a look at the kitten's skin by gently blowing on the fur to create a part. There should be no visible flakiness that would indicate dry skin.

- Gently turn the kitten over on its back and have a look at the "armpits" and under the tail to look for black gravel-like specks called "flea dirt."

If the kitten has a flea or two, you shouldn't think it's a deal breaker or decide on the spot that the cattery is poorly run. Fleas are the plague of every breeder's existence. It's far too easy for them to hitch a ride indoors on someone's pants leg and then the fight is on. This is especially true in areas where the climate is warm year round.

The most important thing is that the kitten not be overrun with fleas. In truly severe infestations, fleas can be responsible for sufficient blood loss to cause anemia. If fleas are present, you want to make sure they're taken care of before you bring the kitten home.

I am categorically against all forms of chemical flea control, no matter how "safe" they are supposed to be. Ask the breeder to bathe the kitten prior to adoption. When you get home, immediately start using a fine tooth flea comb to snag any survivors.

The fleas get caught in the tines of the comb, which you can submerge in a glass of hot, soapy water to kill the parasites. Wash all the kitten's bedding on a daily basis for a week or two to ensure that no flea eggs are allowed to hatch.

- The kitten's eyes should be slightly oval in shape with a sweet and innocent expression that is also bright, curious, and very interested. Make sure there is no evidence of any kind of runny discharge.

- Examine the area around the nostrils. They should be equally free of discharge with no dry encrusted mucous.

The kitten's body should already feel solid, with a good padding of healthy fat over the ribs. You should be able to lightly feel the ribs, but the little cat should be neither emaciated nor obese.

Negotiating the Terms of the Adoption

When both parties are agreed on the adoption, you will be asked to sign a written contract. All catteries have their own adoption agreements, but standard features of the document will include the following:

Preliminary Health Evaluation

It is common for the contract to contain a stipulation that within 48-72 hours a qualified veterinarian should evaluate the kitten's health. You will also be asked to provide written documentation of your compliance with this provision. This establishes a baseline measure of the kitten's condition in case the health guarantee has to be invoked.

Spaying or Neutering Requirement

The vast majority of catteries require that pet quality animals be spayed or neutered before they reach six months of age. To ensure that the procedures are performed, you won't receive the cat's final papers until you provide documentation from the veterinarian.

The intent of the requirement is both to preserve the integrity of the cattery's bloodlines, and to help stem the epidemic of unwanted pets and the tragedy of companion animal homelessness.

Quite often these days, many breeders will already have your kitten neutered and spayed before you collect them.

Strict Prohibitions Against Declawing

Unless the adoption agreement you sign includes strong and pointed language against the inhumane practice of declawing cats, I would be extremely suspicious of the cattery with which you are dealing.

This hideous practice is illegal in Europe and in many parts of the United States, as well it should be. The benign term "declawing" masks the gruesome fact that the procedure necessitates the amputation of the last digit of each of the cat's toes. It is terribly painful and negatively affects the animal's mobility for life, while depriving the cat of its primary means of self-defense.

Maine Coons are no more or less prone to scratching than any other kind of cat, but due to their size, they will need bigger scratching posts or trees. Any cat can be trained to behave appropriately with its claws if provided with the proper apparatus early in life.

I will always maintain the only "justification" for the radical surgical removal of the claws is convenience for the owner. It is not a move designed to support the wellbeing of the cat. And yes, I am extremely passionate about this topic. If you would even consider for one minute having a cat declawed, you have no business keeping one as a pet.

Basic Terms of the Adoption Agreement

In the papers to complete the adoption of a pedigreed Maine Coon, you should see all the following basic provisions and terms:

- The agreed upon price.
- The gender of the kitten and a stipulation about spaying or neutering.
- Any other stipulations regarding the final release of the registration papers.
- The registered names of the breeding pair.
- A description of the specific cat being adopted, including the correct terminology for coat color and pattern if present.
- Complete contact information for both parties entering into the agreement.

Other provisions could include any of the following:

- A promise to provide ongoing health care via the services of a qualified veterinarian, including the administration of recommended vaccinations.

- Stipulation that you understand the grooming requirements of the Maine Coon breed along with an assurance that those requirements will be routinely and appropriately met.

- A promise to contact the breeder should it become necessary for you to give up the cat rather than sell the animal to a third party or surrender it to a shelter.

It's extremely important that you understand that last point. No breeder wants to see one of their cats in a bad living situation or given over to a rescue organization where its fate will either be uncertain, or where it could be euthanized as an unwanted animal.

I cannot emphasize this strongly enough. In the event that you must give up a pedigreed animal, *contact the breeder*. I will always take back one of my cats and either keep the animal or find a way to place it in a new home.

In such a situation, however, I do require that the cat be tested for FELV/FIV, fecal parasites, and ringworm before it comes into my possession. These measures are meant to safeguard my other cats before reintroducing the individual into the population.

The Work of Rescue Groups

Although I touched on the topic of rescue adoptions in Chapter 1, I'd like to return to it now. Do not think for one minute that I am disrespecting the work of rescue groups. In a perfect world, all shelters would be "no kill," but that is not the reality in which we live.

People give up their pets for many reasons. Maine Coon kittens are incredibly adorable and they grow into lovely, even-tempered cats. But in truth, no matter how small they are, all kittens are pretty much rowdy little maniacs. They mistake your leg for a tree trunk and climb right up with those needle-like claws. They merrily topple pot plants, and shower the carpet with litter in their first vigorous attempts to cover the deposit they've just left in the box. Every cat lover has, at one time or another, looked at the destruction a tiny kitten can create and asked, "Why do I do this?"

Of course, the answer is that we're all "crazy cat people" and as maniacal as kittens can be, they're also pure joy wrapped up in a purring little ball of fur. That being said, I have taken in many older rescue animals, including my two crossbred Russian Blues that were abandoned at birth at a vet clinic.

When they moved in with me, they were 11 months old. I missed out on their raucous kittenhood. I have no baby pictures and I am sorry about that. They are stunning adults, and I know they must have been gorgeous babies, but they are also absolutely outstanding cats.

Often, people who think they know what is really involved in having a cat purchase pedigreed animals, including Maine Coons, with the best of intentions and then find that they're in over their heads.

Longhaired cats can be the ones to suffer the most because they are not low maintenance pets. Maine Coons are easier than other breeds, like Persians that can be a constant combing and brushing project, but their coats still need attention.

Even with the concerted efforts of breeders to make sure animals are returned to them, pedigreed cats — in fact, cats of all kinds — are turned over to shelters every day. In other instances, the animals are left alone in the world when their elderly owners die. Pets also suffer economic hardship when families fall on hard times and can no longer afford to care for them.

All rescue animals, regardless of breed, are in need of a "forever home." Of course I'm crazy about Maine Coon cats, but if you are simply looking for a loving companion, please, please, please think about a shelter adoption. You will literally be saving a life.

Even if you do not go this route to acquire your cat, consider supporting the efforts of local no kill shelters, either with your donations or by volunteering. Animal shelters are always in desperate need of funds, supplies, and helping hands.

I can't work in shelters. I want to bring every one of the cats home, and my heart gets broken a hundred times a day. I have tried volunteering, but I can't do it. If, however, you were to flip through my checkbook, the stubs are littered with donations. I'm lucky. I can afford to do that.

But if you can't, there are many other ways to help homeless cats in need:

- Clipping coupons for cat food and litter.
- Buying the items yourself when you do have a few extra dollars and donating them.
- Asking what household supplies, like old towels, are needed at the facility.
- Collecting newspaper to line cages.

You will never know what a shelter can use until you ask. Some groups even hold fundraising garage sales and will take all of your accumulated household junk.

People who work with, and on behalf of, homeless pets perform a vital service in the cause for animal welfare around the world. They are also some of the kindest and most generous folk you will ever meet. Please find a way to help them do what they do so selflessly and with such dedication.

Cost of Buying a Maine Coon

Numerous factors affect the price of a Maine Coon, including availability in a given area and the quality of the cattery's bloodlines.

Although it's a very broad range to throw out, you should expect to pay anywhere from $400 - $1000+ for a pet quality kitten and $1500 and up for a show quality animal. (When you start considering show animals, the prices are typically much higher.)

In the United Kingdom, the price of a pet cat with accredited breeders is now £475 to £500. For breeding and showing, the price is £650 to £850 for a girl or £750 to a £1000 for a boy.

If you cannot afford these prices then consider a Maine Coon rescue or a retired breeding cat. Breeders retire their cats from the breeding program to incorporate new lines, give the cat a chance to live as a pet, the queen is getting too old to continue breeding, the cats are passing along problems, etc. The retired cats usually cost substantially less money than a kitten.

Beware of kittens offered at really low prices with the claim that they are pedigreed Maine Coons. I would seriously doubt that.

The last thing anyone wants to do is to support the unconscionable activities of kitten mills. It's one thing to find someone offering five to six Maine Coon kittens for adoption and another to encounter a "cattery" with a constant supply of low-priced kittens for sale.

Be very suspicious of breeders who tell you to "check back in a few weeks." Reputable catteries only allow their females to deliver litters once or twice per year to minimize the physical stress for the animal. At almost any cattery, you are much more likely to have your name placed on a waiting list.

Also back away from adoptions that are treated as immediate cash sales. Legitimate catteries interview prospective "parents" and seriously evaluate your suitability to provide a good home for the animal.

Chapter 4 - Daily Care for Your Maine Coon

The first thing people ask about any breed of cat they want to adopt is something like, "Do they have a good personality?" What they don't seem to realize is that cats are individuals, too. It's absolutely ridiculous to assume that all cats of the same breed will behave identically under all circumstances.

Animals, like people, are influenced by the manner in which they are raised and the environment in which they live. While it is true that the vast majority of Maine Coons are easygoing, laid back, sociable cats, I knew one woman who was bitterly disappointed when she adopted one that was shy and retiring.

The Maine Coon in question was also the runt of the litter, was adopted from a questionable cattery at too young an age, and taken into a household filled with loud noises without proper socialization — and forced to live with an elderly, very alpha

Siamese who was determined to be an only child!

I have to confess I wasn't all that sympathetic about the woman's complaints, although I did facilitate placing the cat in another home. It was absurd for this person, who in my opinion had no business owning cats at all, to assume that everything was the poor Maine Coon's fault. The animal was completely overwhelmed by its environment and didn't get much, if any, help from its less-than-understanding human!

Some Thoughts on Living With a Maine Coon

Although I completely reject the notion of "one personality fits all" for any breed, I can make a few selective observations about life with a Maine Coon. I do not, however, think it's a good idea to begin a relationship with any animal based on preset expectations. All friendships, including those with companion animals, are strongest when they are allowed to evolve naturally.

Are Cats Selective With Their Affection?

Of course cats are selective with their affections! Aren't you? It is true that some breeds, including the Maine Coon, have a reputation for high sociability. I have found, however, in more than 40 years of living with cats, that all of them have a tendency to single out one person as "theirs." Maine Coons do it, too.

This doesn't mean they aren't fantastic family cats, it just means they're "human" and they do have favorites. If you're that person, you're very lucky! If you're not, you'll still have perfectly delightful interactions with these cordial and good-natured felines.

When you have earned the love and trust of a Maine Coon, they are devoted companions who like to be near their people without getting all clingy. Like most cats, Maine Coons enjoy their lap time, but they're good with camping out on the end of the couch while you read.

They like attention, but they don't get bent out of shape when you're not constantly cooing over them. Basically, this breed leans toward being really well adjusted!

Can a Maine Coon ignore you when you've annoyed him? Absolutely! He's a cat down to the tufts of his toes! But it's extremely rare for a Maine Coon to get bent out of shape enough to really display any temper.

Yes, he might stalk off and be aloof for a bit, but in the end, his native good nature and curiosity will get the best of him and he'll come back in and do something goofy, restoring his good humor and yours in one fell swoop.

Aren't All Cats Loners?

Some cats are loners in that they prefer their one special person and hold themselves apart when visitors are around. The Maine Coon isn't typically one of those cats, however.

Your pet will be glad to see you at the end of the day, but once he knows your schedule, he'll be fine on his own for a few hours while you're at work.

Cats Have Emotional and Physical Needs

Having a cat for a pet involves more than putting out food and water and changing the litter box. A lot of people who adopt a cat for the first time do so with some serious misconceptions about their new pet's real and decided emotional needs.

If you are not prepared to spend time with your Maine Coon, to make him part of the family (even if you're single), to pay for appropriate veterinary care, and to devote the required time to grooming, then reconsider your choice of companion animal.

Bringing Your New Cat Home

One of the things I especially enjoy about Maine Coons is their propensity for being adaptable. They do quite well with other pets, even dogs, and are good with children, simply removing themselves without rancor if something's going on they don't like.

But even given all that, Maine Coons are cats, and like all members of their species, they do like the major parts of their world to stay the same. No cat is ever happy with change.

For this reason, it's important to do a good job managing your kitten's transition from life at the cattery to your household. The move can be intimidating if not handled correctly, and disaster can ensue in two vital aspects of feline life: the litter box and the food bowl.

The Transitional Litter Box

The kitten you adopt should be accustomed to using a litter pan, but cats are incredibly particular about their "bathrooms." You need to make sure that you don't do anything to confuse a young cat and set back its training in this regard.

Find out the type of box and litter the breeder has been using with the cat and replicate the arrangement exactly. When the kitten first moves into your home, keep it confined to a limited area and provide it with one litter box.

As you gradually allow the cat to have the run of the house, consider providing a second box. The general rule of thumb is to have one more pan than there are cats in the house.

If, at any point, you decide to use a different type of litter box or litter, make the change very slowly and don't discard the original items until your cat is comfortable with the new arrangement and doing his "business" there routinely.

The Transitional Menu

In the matter of your kitten's food bowl, again, find out what the breeder has been using and present your new cat with exactly the same type of bowl and the same food. The last thing you want is to trigger some kind of gastrointestinal upset.

The breeder will likely have good suggestions about how the kitten's diet should change as it grows. You can also discuss food choices with your vet, and I will be talking more about nutrition shortly. Just remember that all cats are carnivores. The quality of any food that doesn't list meat as the main ingredient should be considered suspect.

Have plenty of toys waiting for your new baby. Pay attention to what the cat does and doesn't like. These observations will guide your future purchases. Just make sure that none of the items present a choking hazard. Don't bother with catnip. Kittens don't react to "kitty weed" before the age of 6-9 months.

Starting a Grooming Routine

Although I will go into much more detail about grooming, you should start a combing and brushing routine with your Maine Coon kitten immediately. The breeder will already have been doing this with the cat and it's imperative that you not fall down on the schedule.

Find out the type of implements the breeder has been using and when and under what conditions the grooming has been done. If the kitten is used to sitting on someone's lap in the evenings for the brushing, do the same thing.

With every element of the kitten's daily routine — litter box, diet, and grooming — you are trying to emphasize continuity and giving the baby a sense of "life as usual."

Take the Breeder's Guidance

Even if you see yourself as an old hand with cats, take the breeder's guidance in creating a successful transition for the kitten. The breeder doesn't just know the Maine Coon breed, but also knows the young cat now in your care.

Most breeders, myself included, recommend keeping kittens in a small segregated area for a few days until they get comfortable in their new home. This is an especially good idea if there are other pets in the house, so that introductions can be made via paws under the door and a lot of exploratory sniffing.

When face-to-face meetings are attempted for the first time, it's important for you not to overreact to any trash talk or half-hearted paw slaps that take place. Animals pick up on our emotions and, without meaning to, you could negatively influence the whole interaction.

Animals in multi-pet households work out their own pecking order. Even as young cats, Maine Coons are calm and genial by nature, but they still have claws. In kittens, those claws are sharp as needles. Don't be surprised if it's your older cat that backs away yelping after getting nailed by a slap from a little hissing ball of fur. (Try not to laugh. It's embarrassing enough for your older cat as is!)

Clearly, if these first meetings get out of hand you'll need to intervene, but after about a week to 10 days everything should be settled down. Once the kitten is ready to venture into the larger parts of the house, however, you will need to make sure you've kitten proofed those areas.

Kitten Proofing

Kittens, tiny though they are, are a force with which to be reckoned. Their bravery and curiosity far outweighs their common sense. A baby cat has absolutely no understanding of just how little he is. Kittens see themselves as fearless lions and will try to tackle anything with no regard for the consequences.

So, for starters, get down on the floor at kitten level. Look around and imagine what looks like fun and interesting "trouble" to get yourself into and start your kitten proofing efforts there.

For instance, see that dangling cord attached to the TV? Wouldn't it be fun to give that a good yank? Tape that and any and all other cords down (and while you're at it, cap the electrical outlets). Cords represent not only an electrocution danger, but are also the avenue by which very heavy objects can be sent crashing to the floor.

Remove all houseplants. I personally have a "no plants allowed" policy because so many are toxic to cats. If you do want to keep your plants, research their toxicity and position them either out of reach or in areas where your cat isn't allowed to go.

Use baby latches on cabinet doors to secure them against clever little paws. This is an especially important precaution in cabinets where any kind of household chemicals are stored.

Learning Fluency in "Cat"

The extent to which a Maine Coon uses its voice is completely individualistic, but overall, this is a chatty breed given to melodic chirping and trilling. They are conversational, but pleasantly so, and not at all raucous.

I'd like to be able to give you a dictionary for "cat," but their language is not limited to vocalizations. It's a complex mixture of signals comprising expressions, body language, scents, and sounds.

Language experts guess that cats can pick up a working vocabulary of about 25-30 words from us, but they can emit about 100 sounds of their own. Just as a basis for comparison, it's estimated that dogs learn around 100 words, yet they make only 15 sounds. That theorizing is all well and good, but I wonder if those experts have ever actually lived with a cat or a dog.

I work from home and spend an enormous amount of time talking to my cats. I assure you they know far more than 25-30 words. The real issue in communicating with a cat isn't his comprehension but rather a matter of how you get his attention.

These animals don't ignore us because they are by nature arrogant. While it's true that you've never really *been* ignored until you've been ignored by a cat, the real reason Fluffy doesn't hang on your every word is that he may not be able to hear what you're saying.

Cats do have very acute hearing, but it's designed to pick up high-pitched sounds, like a mouse squeaking behind the wall on the other side of the living room. Cats often don't pay attention to us when we talk to them because much of human speech drops below the frequencies their ears are built to pick up on.

To them, we must sound like little more than a dull roar. Yelling at a cat gets you nowhere, but watch what happens when you whisper. His ears will go up, his eyes will dilate, and he'll look right at you. Pair soft-voiced commands with hand signals that capitalize on a cat's instinct to learn body language and you'll be shocked at how effective your "commands" will be.

You can try your sternest voice when you tell a Maine Coon or any other cat to get "down," but in all likelihood you'll be confronted with an impassive and vaguely bored stare. But say the word "down" softly and punctuate it by sternly pointing at the floor and Fluffy will generally do as you ask.

Do not, however, assume that your cats can't or won't pick up on and learn your spoken language. Again, you must remember that all cats are *individuals*. I had a gray and white American Shorthair tom with a vocabulary so extensive, I often caught him responding to things I said to someone else over the telephone.

I do believe that my cats and I "converse" unusually well. I spend a lot of time with them and I do talk to them. (Yes, I do realize this sounds a little daft.) But I think the more you expose an intelligent animal to any type of communication — whether it be words or hand signals — the more you both will learn about how the other communicates. After all, the word "communication" does imply a two-way exchange of information, so you have some things to learn as well.

To that end, let's consider some of the fundamentals of speaking "cat."

- A cat with wide-open eyes and small pupils is calm and interested.
- The same wide-eyed cat with large pupils is afraid.
- When a cat's eyes go "hard" he's not only interested, but also focused, and likely ready to pounce on something he sees as "prey."
- Narrowed eyes paired with a lashing tail and ears that are back and flat clearly signal a warning, "Back off."
- A cat striding along with his tail flipped up and forward

is relaxed and in a good mood.

When Maine Coons do use their voices, they don't typically let out the kind of multi-octave yowls you'll hear from one of the Oriental breeds that literally raise the hairs on the back of your neck.

There are two sounds that all cats make that I really love. The first is one you'll hear most often when your pet is sitting with face pressed to the window, staring at a bird or a squirrel. It's sort of a chattering teeth clacking, often accompanied with a short little bark. It's basically cat for, "Wow! Mom! Look!"

And that signature "meow" that you think is your cat speaking to you? Uh. Okay. Brace yourself. Adult cats don't meow at one another, so when your cat does send a meow in your direction, it's treating you like a kitten in need of placation or correction. Yes, our cats really do see us that way!

Litter Box Management

One reason cats are so popular as companions is the fact that they can live inside and take care of their elimination needs in a pan of sand or gravel. Not only does kitty not have to be taken for walks outside, he'd have no part of such nonsense anyway.

(That's actually something of a myth. Many cats, Maine Coons included, will agreeably walk on a leash if the training is begun at an early age. Outfit your cat with a harness, rather than a collar, if you want to teach it to walk on a lead.)

Litter Box Training

Your kitten should come to you litter box trained so that your primary responsibility is one of maintenance and reinforcing good habits. If, however, you do have to introduce a kitten to a litter box, the process goes something like this.

- Fill a pan with sand or gravel litter.
- Put the kitten in the pan.
- Gently take its front paws and make a digging motion for a few strokes.

The cat will take it from there. By nature cats are absolutely fastidious creatures. They come pre-programmed to dig, do their business, and cover. Show them where they have soft "dirt" to do that and the rest is pure instinct on their part.

The Potential for Litter Box Problems

Many cats are given up for problems related to litter box use, a fact that causes me equal parts aggravation and sadness — know that there is always a reason (medical, environmental, or psychological) for a change in litter habits.

Cats are so clean by nature that if they go "off" their litter pan the cause is likely a physical problem, like a urinary infection or a bladder blockage. The first step in addressing the issue is to take the cat to the vet!

Reason through the issue like a cat. You go into the pan to do what you need to do. It hurts. In cat logic, you try to find a place next time that doesn't hurt! The cat associates the location with the pain, and tries to avoid the pain.

If there is no physical ailment, then consider your own responsibility for what's happened. If you aren't doing a good job of maintaining the box, the cat may be refusing to use the site because it's just too disgusting.

Humans have roughly 5 million receptors for odor sensing. Cats have 200 million. If you think something smells offensive, to a cat it's absolutely repugnant. Is it any wonder he doesn't want to go in a filthy litter box?

Also consider if you've changed anything about the box itself. Have you switched litters or gone from an open tray to a covered one? Cats have very definite preferences about such things. It's never a good idea to make sudden changes to their normal set-up.

New litters should be slowly mixed with the old, gradually phasing out the type you are discontinuing. New boxes should be placed beside the old one until the animal is comfortable with the new arrangement. Abrupt changes typically result in abrupt reactions.

When changing litters to a completely different type, (clay to clumping, or heavy clumping to something much lighter, like corn-based World's Best Kitty Litter), another method is two litter boxes side by side. Become a little lax in keeping the old litter box quite as clean as the new, and the cat will naturally migrate to the new, cleaner litter box.

What to Do When Accidents Happen

If your Maine Coon does go outside the litter pan, don't discipline the cat. Just get to work. You have some serious cleaning to do to prevent a recurrence. Remember, cats live in a world where scent is a major sensory experience.

When a cat urinates or defecates in a particular spot, in the future his nose will tell him that is now an acceptable place to "go." It is imperative that all traces of odor be removed, with specialized enzymatic cleaners, after such accidents.

I especially like a line of products for this purpose made by Nature's Miracle. They work exceedingly well and are affordably priced at $5 - $10 / £3 - £6 per bottle.

Available Types of Litter

The traditional clay-based gravel is far from the only option now available to cat owners, but it is still very cheap, selling for just $2.50 - $5.00 (£2-£4) per 10 lbs. (4.53 kg). Frankly, however, clay isn't ideal. It generates a terrific amount of dust and doesn't do a good job of absorbing urine, instead allowing wet puddles to accumulate in the bottom of the pan, which over time seep into the plastic. This creates an excessive ammonia odor that ultimately cannot be removed, and the wet litter is a real mess to clean up.

The preferred option for most cat people today is a clumping sand litter, which is both soft in texture and far less likely to cause "tracking" problems.

Old-style clay litters had a tendency to cling to the cat's feet and come off once the animal exits the box. This occurs less with sand, but vigorous scratchers can send plumes of the stuff flying, so be forewarned.

Clumping litters come in several different types, including multiple-cat, odor control, and low dust — or some combination thereof. If you use sand, get a covered litter box to help keep the material more contained and consider putting the box on a rug or mat that you can carry outside and shake out from time to time.

Do not put clumps from the litter box in the toilet for flushing unless the box specifically says the material is "flushable." Otherwise, the litter will essentially harden to concrete in the pipes and utterly destroy your plumbing.

Although clumping litters are more expensive, they also return higher value in terms of efficiency, absorbency, and odor control. The litters are readily available in markets and grocery stores, selling for $18 / £12 for 42 lbs. (19 kg).

I know some people who have attempted to switch their cats over to plant-based, eco-friendly litters that are biodegradable. I wholeheartedly applaud the concept, but my cats won't use the stuff at all.

These litters, which may be made of ground corn cobs or some type of wood shavings, are very lightweight. I don't think they feel substantial enough to the cat, plus the litter clings to the cat's fur. My cats were clearly annoyed by this fact and they proceeded to scatter the stuff all over the house.

Shaved pine is one example of an eco-friendly litter, selling for $10 / £7 per 20 lbs. (9.07 kg). I suppose if a cat were introduced to the material at a young age it might work, but I've had no success getting my cats to "go green."

Another biodegradable product, amorphous silica gel, is relatively new. The absorbent crystals in these products are intended to prevent urine puddles by trapping and absorbing the liquid, and also inhibiting bacterial growth.

This is not a product I've tried personally, but several of my friends report that the texture is similar to that of gravel. Their cats were receptive to the crystals, which do exhibit superior absorbency over clumping litters. On average, you will pay $16 / £11 for 8 lbs.

Selecting a Litter Box

There are three standard litter box configurations. In order of expense they are: open pan, covered box, and electric self-scooping.

Open plastic pans cost only $6 - $10 / £4 - £6 and have been used for years. It doesn't have to be a "litter box" from a pet store. You could even use a dishpan or a higher-sided plastic box/bin. The two major disadvantages to this approach are unsightliness and the mess created by digging and covering. Some cats won't use anything else, however, so you are faced with using litter trapping mats and placing the box in an out-of-the-way location or behind a screen.

Covered pans are far tidier and easier to place. For cats that prefer a sense of privacy, the arrangement is ideal. The vented lids include filters that help to control dust, but tracking and the occasional plume of litter out the entrance can still be problematic.

Another disadvantage is that, because owners don't see them, they are not likely to be cleaned as often. Covered litter boxes also trap in aromas which some cats don't like. Many cats just prefer their boxes to be open.

These boxes can be purchased in almost any configuration, from standard rectangles to triangles that fit neatly in corners. Size and shape determine price, but most fall in a range of $30 - $50 / £20 - £33.

Basically every cat owner sees a self-scooping box for the first time and wants it immediately. I bought one as soon as they came out. The idea is fantastic, and the boxes do work, but to be honest, the reception among my cats was mixed.

The function of the box works around a motion sensor triggered by the cat exiting the box. The signal activates a rake or a similar mechanism that combs through the used clumping litter to capture and remove the waste material, which is dumped into a closed receptacle.

When the bin is full, you empty it or throw the whole thing

away. The unit I purchased used disposable plastic boxes with lids. (Not great, environmentally, but a very contained solution.)

The box absolutely traumatized my youngest male. He would have no part of the "monster" and insisted on using a "normal" box. My "middle" boy was utterly fascinated. He came galloping to watch every time the elderly female used the box, which created a diplomatic situation because she demanded complete privacy.

We did continue to use the box, and subsequent cats that have been introduced to it as kittens are perfectly fine with it. Given that, if you want to go this route, introduce your cats to the automatic box as early in life as possible. Expect to pay $150 - $200 (£98 - £130) for one of these units.

Tidy Cats Breeze Litter Box System

If you have the budget for it, I highly recommend the Tidy Cats Breeze Litter Box System which retails for about $30. This gets you one litter box, one scoop, one bag of pellets, and four pads. You obviously have to factor in the ongoing cost of the unique pellets.

The advantage in this system is that odors are greatly reduced because the hard clay pellets do not absorb moisture. So instead, the urine drains straight down through a grid to the pad (in its own slide-out drawer), leaving the solid waste on top to be easily scooped away.

Interaction and Play

Maine Coons love to bat things around on the floor, but they aren't big jumpers and climbers. This varies by individual, and most I've known love to stand up and go after dangling toys on wands. Because they have a reputation for being "dog-like," they're generally up for a game of fetch and I've had several that go crazy for the "red dot" of a laser pointer toy.

Toys to avoid include bells that might detach and be swallowed, and feathers, as the quill can become stuck in a cat's throat if they chew them. Watch out for toys that dangle from elastic strings.

Uncooked pasta makes a great toy, as well as ping pong balls, a rolled up sock, practice golf balls (lightweight, plastic, with holes in them) and rolled up tin foil or paper.

Primarily, a Maine Coon is just happy to be spending time with you. I always counsel new cat parents, regardless of the breed they've adopted, to just watch your pet and get to know what interests and intrigues him. It's not a huge problem for a few introductory toys to go ignored until you find just the right thing. I have one male who thinks a crumpled up grocery store receipt on a hardwood floor is the best cat toy ever!

Maine Coons are not aloof loners. They're goofy pals. They'll show you what they like and don't like. They're just as capable of being stubborn as any other cat, but they tend to be fairly nice about it. This is, however, an extremely intelligent breed and they respond well to learning routines and "tricks."

That should not, however, be a forced thing. I don't advocate presenting any cat with a class schedule of "tricks," and then trying to get him to study and pass the test. That just doesn't go well in my experience. I prefer to get to know my cats and then create both games and tricks that match the individual's interests and tastes.

One of my smartest cats turned doorknobs with his paws, and loved for me to close the bedroom door so he could prove it to me — over and over again.

Another liked a version of the old "shell game." He had an exceptional memory and was adept at opening boxes. I'd show him a toy, then turn around and hide the item in one of several boxes. Invariably he'd walk straight to the right box and retrieve the toy. It was almost spooky. Like most cats, his attention span lasted about 15 minutes and then it was time for a nap, but he never tired of playing the game one more time.

Rewarding positive behavior is the foundation of all animal training. With a Maine Coon, the reward is typically just being with you. They are incredibly loyal companions and are very affectionate. Just spend time interacting with and getting to know your cats. The games and tricks will evolve naturally.

The Matter of Scratching

Cats will scratch. It's a fact of life with a feline. Maine Coons don't have a reputation for being especially destructive with their claws, but they are big cats and will need big scratching posts. Understand that cats are not being bad when they scratch. They have an instinctual need to clean and sharpen their claws. With the right training, this is no more an issue than litter box management, but part of the responsibility does fall to you.

A simple scratching pole that costs $30 / £20 will generally suffice, but you need to buy the tallest, sturdiest one in the store. I confess that all of mine have access to elaborate cat trees with perches, tunnels, ramps, and observation platforms. These units set me back $100 - $300 (£65 - £197) each, but they're worth it in my opinion for their high interest level and added exercise value.

When problem-scratching of furniture is an issue, I recommend applying either pennyroyal or orange essence spray as a deterrent. Remember, cats have fantastically acute noses and they hate both of these scents. I've used both and have not had any trouble with fabric staining, but always perform a test application on a small, unobtrusive area first. Each of these mixtures sells for $12 - $15 / £7.87 - £9.84.

Catnip encourages scratching, so be sure to keep catnip away from upholstered furniture and carpet. DO rub catnip on the scratching post from time to time.

The corrugated cardboard scratchers are inexpensive and excellent, impregnated with catnip. Posts wrapped in sisal rope are an even better and sturdier choice.

One of my adopted Maine Coons clearly had a carpet scratching habit. I acquired a small carpet sample in a contrasting color, and she immediately switched to scratching on it and never bothered the carpet or sofa again.

Double-sided adhesive strips are also an excellent and affordable deterrent for scratching because cats dislike the "tacky" feeling on their paws. The strips sell for around $8 - $10 / £5.25 - $6.56.

Photo Credit: Robin Warren of Red Flannel Cattery

Chapter 5 – Feeding Your Maine Coon

Like many "facts" about cats, the idea that all felines are finicky eaters is greatly overblown. They have likes and dislikes just like us. I'd sooner starve than choke down a Brussels sprout and I have one male cat that will stare fixedly at that nasty, chunky mess in the bowl until you replace it with proper, smooth pâté.

Photo Credit: Riley, 26 pounds and 3 years old in the photo, born and bred at Megacoon Cattery

Yes, texture matters just that much to a cat, as does scent. A cat will not eat what he cannot smell. If a cat has a cold or his sinuses are stopped up from seasonal allergies, the vet often prescribes giving the animal the smelliest food imaginable to stimulate its appetite. I've even had to feed mine cheap sardines that absolutely reek.

Refusing food under these circumstances isn't being "picky." It's a finally honed survival instinct that prevents these small carnivores from ingesting anything that might make them sick. By odor alone cats know what is and isn't good for them to consume. They won't touch any food that smells wrong to them or that has no scent at all.

Never try to starve a cat into eating something he doesn't want. In the first place, it won't work, but beyond that the strategy is cruel and unhealthy for the animal. If a cat suddenly refuses food he's always accepted happily, find out what's wrong, including taking the animal in for a vet checkup.

The problem could be anything from a cold to dental pain. I inherited a psychotic Himalayan from my late aunt several years ago. The breed has a lovely reputation, but Ming didn't get the memo. The cranky little beast suddenly refused the one food she had loudly demanded for 12 years and I became worried, even though she was an impossible member of the household.

I called the vet and took her in. When the doctor looked in Ming's mouth, the poor thing had two abscessed teeth in need of extraction. I'd be ill tempered under those circumstances, too!

Emphasize High-Quality Foods

Although it may not seem like a helpful or very specific thing to say, my honest advice it to buy the best cat food you can afford, which means those with meat as a primary ingredient. Cats are carnivores. The cheaper the food, the higher the content of grain-based fillers, which constitutes lesser quality feline nutrition.

It can also be false economy, because your cat will feel hungry when he is not getting the required nutrition. It passes through their system without having much effect. So you end up spending more, by feeding more frequently!

Good quality foods have both high protein and fat content, with only a small percentage of carbohydrates required for your Maine Coon's diet (about 5%).

The inclusion of Taurine, Niacin, and Vitamin A are excellent signs of a good food, approved by AAFCO. This stands for Association of American Feed Control Officials. This non-profit organization sets standards for pet food in the USA.

Fish, such as tuna, also contains excellent nutrients — but this should only be a small part of a balanced diet.

Grow cat grass in a pot. The folic acid helps prevent anemia.

Canned pumpkin works like yogurt does for people, by calming the lining of the intestines down and firming up loose stool.

Offer Wet and Dry Food

Cats thrive on a well-balanced diet that contains a mix of both wet and dry food. It is a myth that there's less litter box mess if wet foods are eliminated. Wet foods are a critical moisture source for cats and an important element of weight control.

Any cat, including a Maine Coon, will start to pack on the pounds eating nothing but high calorie dry food. The breed is large anyway, so it's easy to be fooled that your tubby tabby is perfectly normal. Even with a longhaired cat, you should be able to look at the body shape from above and see a slight indentation behind the ribs and just before the hips begin. If you can't see or feel this indentation, your cat is getting too fat.

It's also helpful to weigh your pet periodically and to make note of the number. Sudden weight gain or loss is an indicator of potential illness.

Just be careful to check the ingredients of any dry food, as some are excessively high in carbohydrates, which isn't doing your cat an awful lot of good, to be honest.

The positive with dry food, however, is that many people believe it helps clean the teeth, leading to less dental decay. Some vets, however, will disagree, saying there is no evidence for this. Other vets do believe it helps.

Avoid All Human Food!

Like most cats, some Maine Coons could care less about human food, while others will beg plaintively in those funny little voices of theirs. The point is not to let them develop a taste for table scraps and treats in the first place. Any breed will become a demanding beggar if given the opportunity.

No domestic cat should be allowed to become obese. Being overweight puts your pet at risk for numerous health problems, including arthritis and diabetes. Large boned cats like the Maine Coon are prone to hip dysplasia.

Don't court even more serious joint-related problems by allowing Fluffy to be a junk-food junkie. Maybe you're no good at controlling what you eat, but you can certainly do better by your cat!

Schedules and Portions

I've never been much of one to carefully measure out portions for my cats, unless I have an individual with a weight problem. One of my favorite domestic shorthairs was just rotund by nature. He was adorable, sweet, and packed on pounds just looking at food. He's the only cat I've ever owned who simply could not lose weight no matter what the vet and I tried.

Typically, I've always allowed my cats to free feed on dry food after they're a year old. (Free feeding just means leaving dry food out at all times.) Once they've grazed through roughly one cup (118 grams) of kibble in a day, however, I don't refill the bowl.

I'm fine giving kittens a second scoop in the afternoon because they burn up so much energy, but with adult cats I prefer their main meals to be two servings of wet food dispensed in the morning and early evening. For the average cat the servings come out to about 5.5 ounces (14.17 grams), but if you have a really big Maine Coon with no weight issues, you can double that.

Photo Credit: Kat Doring of Kats Kits

Foods That are Toxic to Cats

Clearly, human food is not good for keeping a cat at a normal weight, but there are also many things we eat that are toxic to felines. Do not ever give your cat:

- any form of alcohol including beer
- grapes or raisins
- chocolate
- onions or chives
- raw eggs
- avocados
- yeast dough

Note that, although raw eggs could be harmful for cats, I have often fed my Maine Coons left over scrambled eggs. Eggs are also in most kitten Glop recipes. Glop is often used to supplement kittens, older cats, and sick cats.

Often cats find coffee tempting, especially when it's laced with cream and sugar. Don't let your cat get away with this, or allow it anywhere near chocolate. Caffeine can be deadly to cats, and the cacao seeds used to make chocolate include methylxanthines, which are also present in soda.

These chemicals cause life-threatening symptoms including:

- excessive thirst and dehydration
- vomiting and diarrhea
- heart palpitations and arrhythmia
- seizures and tremors

Also beware of artificial sweeteners, especially those containing xylitol, which causes liver failure in cats.

Cats and the Milk Myth

As much as it's taken as a matter of "common knowledge," the idea that cats need milk or cream is really just a myth. I'm not saying your Maine Coon *won't* lap up either dairy product, but they don't *need* the stuff, and it really isn't very good for them.

Why? Well, think about it. Cow's milk is for cows. It can actually be harmful to cats. Ask anyone you know how uncomfortable it is to be lactose intolerant and you'll understand how severe the gastrointestinal upset can be. Many cats experience exactly the same thing because their bodies don't produce enough of the enzyme lactase.

Milk isn't all that great for us either, no matter what the milk industry might have you believe. Every living mammal produces milk that is appropriate for its own young. We aren't calves any more than cats are!

As an occasional treat, there's nothing wrong with offering your cat a dish of milk, but if there are any signs of gastrointestinal upset — including an especially smelly deposit in the litter box — don't repeat the experiment.

Understanding Your Cat's Preferences

Discuss food selection with the breeder and with your vet, but also understand that cats have their likes and dislikes, which may have absolutely nothing to do with taste. You will need to learn to cater to these idiosyncrasies.

Texture preference can be hugely important in getting a cat to eat properly and well. I have one tom that loves beef pâté food. Offer him chunky beef, however, and he flicks his tail and stalks away.

With Maine Coons, you also have to be aware of the effect of whisker stress. The breed has long, luxuriant whiskers and many don't like to reach into deep food bowls. The sensation of their whiskers dragging on the sides of the bowl is uncomfortable to them.

If your cat routinely drops chunks of food out on the floor to eat, whisker stress is probably the culprit. The problem can certainly affect how much the animal eats, but is easily solved with a special tray-like cat bowl. These units are somewhat expensive. They sell for $25 / £16 as compared to regular food and water containers priced at $5 - $10 / £3 - £7, but your cat's nutritional intake will be better and you won't have messy clumps of food on the floor any more.

I would avoid plastic food or water dishes because plastic is porous and can harbor bacteria. Because of this, plastic dishes can cause "chin acne." Glass, metal, or sealed pottery/china is preferable.

Until you find a high-quality food that your cat will eat reliably and sort out all of his individual preferences, don't buy in bulk. Also, some cats happily eat the same foods daily, while others demand variety. You'll want to buy accordingly.

Budgeting for Cat Food Purchases

I completely understand the desire to have a good idea of the cost of keeping an animal, but nailing down some budgetary items like food is all but impossible. There are simply too many brands on the market.

Based purely on my own experience, I would offer a conservative estimate of $75 / £45 per month on wet and dry food combined. The wet food will take up roughly a third of that budget, as it is always more expensive.

Natural or Alternative Dietary Options

Especially since the reported deaths of both dogs and cats from contaminated commercial foods, many pet owners have become interested in alternative or natural diets. This also speaks to a growing awareness of the potential dangers of chemicals and additives in highly processed products.

The most popular of the natural feeding programs for pets is a plan commonly referred to as the raw diet. I don't use it with my pets, but I am not making any recommendations for or against the approach, only offering basic information to my readers.

If you consider using this feeding program, it is imperative that you understand how much more is involved in preparing the food correctly, rather than just putting some uncooked meat in your pet's bowl.

The idea behind the raw diet is the notion that domesticated companion animals will thrive when they eat what they would acquire for themselves if they were allowed to hunt naturally. Since cats are carnivores, this means giving them food that replicates a fresh carcass — including bones.

Most veterinarians, and many cat breeders, myself included, have heard more than enough right there. Bones create a serious choking hazard and can easily lacerate a cat's throat, stomach, and intestines. Additionally, the raw diet also increases the risk of salmonella poisoning.

The food must be handled meticulously in a spotless kitchen, with equipment reserved specifically for this purpose only. Use nothing but raw chicken and beef, *never* pork. All unused food must be discarded after 2-3 days, even if it has been refrigerated, and none of the food should ever be microwaved.

Nothing I have said here is sufficient instruction to begin feeding your pets a raw diet. You must learn the precise preparation methods, acquire the correct equipment, and use only the proper food combinations to achieve the necessary balance of vitamins and minerals.

NEVER begin a raw feeding program or make any other major alteration in your pet's diet without first consulting with your veterinarian and/or breeder.

The Importance of Hydration

Keeping your cats well-hydrated with a constant supply of clean, fresh water is a crucial part of good husbandry. Wipe out the water container daily to prevent the build-up of bacteria, and consider acquiring a drinking fountain to encourage better consumption in volume. Many cats won't drink from a stagnant dish.

Photo Credit: Sharon Stegall of Dracoonfly Maine Coon Cattery

Cat water fountains also carry the added advantage of changeable filters, which is excellent for areas with poor water quality. The units cost $30 / £23 on average and, from my experience, last at least two years.

Chapter 6 - Grooming Your Maine Coon

Although Maine Coons are not as hard to groom as other longhaired breeds, they do need to be brushed and occasionally bathed to keep their fur free of accumulations of oil, grit, and dander. A lot of these tasks are easily performed at home, but it's only realistic to expect to require the periodic services of a professional groomer.

The Feline Temperament and Grooming

Professional groomers class cats in three temperamental ranges when it comes to accepting being handled and bathed.

- *Shy cats* find the grooming process frightening and must be reassured steadily and constantly. They don't tend to be aggressive, but they do try very hard to escape the whole business.

- *Compliant cats* are totally agreeable to grooming and may even enjoy it. They're not aggressive, are easy to handle, and put up no complaint whatsoever. Most Maine Coons fall into this category.

- *Aggressive cats* pretty much lose their minds. They can't be groomed at home, and may even require light tranquilization or actual sedation at the groomer's or vet clinic.

Clearly, the sooner a cat becomes used to being groomed, the more tolerant he'll be throughout his life.

Maine Coons have silky fur that is not as prone to tangling and matting as that of a Persian. Comb your cat several times a week with a shedding comb to remove loose hair and minor mats and tangles.

Shedding combs have two sets of adjacent wire teeth with one set longer than the other. My favorites are made by Coastal Pet Safari which retail for less than $10 / £6.12.

You never want to allow any longhaired cat to develop mats that will block airflow to the skin and potentially cause itching and then infection from skin damage, due to scratching.

Don't try to remove any mats that do form. Your pet's skin is very fragile and easily wounded. Minor mats can be gently teased apart with your fingers, but you must *never try to cut out a mat*. The risk of injury is too great. Under those circumstances, the services of a professional groomer are absolutely required.

Claw Clipping

Whether you are grooming your cat or a professional is

undertaking the task, the first step is always to clip the cat's claws — to at least bring its natural "weapons" down to a manageable level.

Get kittens used to this at a young age. It's not the clipping itself that feels weird to a kitten, it's the exposing of the nail. So when you are cuddling your new kitten on your lap, play with the paws and expose the nails (without doing any clipping) so that this feels like a normal thing to do. Kittens' claws should be clipped every week, adults every two weeks.

Maine Coons tend to be very compliant with all of these chores. Place the cat in your lap and pick up one front paw. Use your thumb to gently apply pressure just behind the toes so the claws will extend. The curved tips are translucent, but the vascular "quick" at the base is pink.

Be careful not to clip into this area. Not only would that cause your pet pain, but it would also result is excessive bleeding. Snip off the sharp points only and don't forget the dewclaw on the side of the foot.

I suggest following a philosophy of "less restraint." Cats don't like to feel trapped and held down. Just make sure the animal is secure in your lap. As you get more experienced with claw clipping, the chore will go quickly so the cat won't really have time to get upset.

Buy a small pair of clippers designed for use with pets. I like the ones with handles, like those on pliers. The grip is better, more controlled, and the price is reasonable at around $10 / £6.

The Tail Test for Bathing

If you've never given a cat a bath, and if you have no idea how your cat will react to being bathed, use the "tail test" to judge the animal's tolerance. By dragging your pet's tail through the water briefly, you will see whether he has an issue with being wet. Provided your cat doesn't go ballistic, you should be able to move forward with the bath without issue.

Use the same kind of preliminary testing if you plan on using a blow dryer. Start at the cat's tail and try working up. If the cat thinks it's being attacked by a "cat-eating monster" you'll know it in a heartbeat.

Actual Bathing

Always have everything you need on hand and nearby. Work with water that is lukewarm to slightly warm. Be careful not to allow water to get in the cat's ears, eyes, or nose. If possible, gently place cotton balls in the ears to ensure they stay dry.

Never pour water over the cat's face. Clean that area with a warm washcloth, but don't use soap. Cats' eyes are extremely sensitive to chemical irritation.

Degreasing

When the animal is thoroughly wet, there are two stages to a proper bath for a long-haired cat: degreasing and shampooing.

Find a degreasing formula specifically designed for use with pets. The substance is a paste-like gel applied and rinsed as if it were a shampoo. Degreasers cost around $15 / £9.19 for 16 ounces / 454 grams.

Shampoo

Pick a natural, scent-free shampoo that is hypoallergenic. Most of these products come in 16 ounce / 454 gram bottles or larger, retailing for $10 - $15 / £6.12 - £9.19.

Work the shampoo into the fur gently. Don't scrub, as this will lead to tangling. Always over-rinse so there's no residue left in the fur, then drain all the water out of the tub and run your hands through the coat in straight motions to further remove the excess.

Swaddle the cat in a soft dry towel. Use drying strokes following the natural direction of the fur. Don't scrub!

Blow Drying

Blow-drying is typically the home grooming deal breaker. If your cat reacts poorly to the vacuum cleaner, don't expect the blow dryer to go over well. If, however, your cat is compliant, blow in the direction of the fur while brushing in the same direction. Use the lowest setting possible. You may need help with the belly and legs.

Clipping and Trimming

If any clipping or trimming needs to be done, hire a professional. In areas that get very warm in the summer, you may opt to give your Maine Coon a "lion cut" for the animal's comfort. The "cut" actually involves shaving the body, leaving cuffs on the feet and a mane at the neck.

Ear Care

Really serious ear cleaning is a job for the groomer or veterinarian. At home I don't do more than use a cotton ball dipped in warm water to swab the flap and the opening to the ear canal. Never use a cotton swab.

If you can see black, tarry debris and detect a yeasty smell, the cat likely has ear mites and will need to see the vet. The animal's ears will need a thorough cleaning and you will have to apply topical cream to kill the parasites.

Photo Credit: Mareen Holden-Ritchie of Amoramist Maine Coons

Finding a Professional Groomer

On average, I'd say a Maine Coon should be professionally groomed about four times a year. If the cat isn't cooperative with home grooming, more trips to a professional will be necessary. I am a huge fan of groomers who will come to you to work, with your pet at home where the cat feels most secure and comfortable.

If you do have to transport the cat to a groomer, be sure to use a sound travel crate. Never allow the cat to be loose in the car!

You can ask your breeder for a reference for a good local groomer or ask at your vet clinic. Also check the office bulletin board. Make sure that any groomer with whom you work has prior experience with Maine Coon cats.

I suggest that you visit the grooming facility without your pet. Ask for a tour and get a clear sense of how your pet will be handled while on the premises. Pay special attention to the work areas and how they are maintained.

Photo Credit: Robin Warren of Red Flannel Cattery

Specifically ask if all animals that enter the establishment are required to be current with their vaccinations. Since so many feline diseases can be communicated with nothing more than a nose tap, what precautions are taken to keep the cats strictly separated?

Grooming costs vary widely, but on average, a session should cost around $50 / £30.64.

Cat Crate

The all-important cat crate for travel and transport is not an item on which you want to scrimp. Get a quality crate that has a strong latch and fasteners. Whether you decide for a soft or hard-sided travel box, the price should still fall in a range of $25 - $50 / £15 - £30. This can, of course, vary by size and brand.

I also strongly recommend a crate that opens on the top as well as the side, unless you have a large Maine Coon. If so, this type of box is unlikely to be sturdy enough to support the cat's weight. If you ever have a cat that is injured or sick, you can gently cradle the cat in a towel and lower him/her through the top, and then remove the cat the same way at the vet — way easier and less stressful than side loading.

Crates that have a door at the top don't cost more, and they also provide better ventilation and better visibility for the owner.

Chapter 7 - Your Maine Coon Cat's Health

Maine Coons are marvelously healthy cats. There are only two genetic conditions associated with the breed: hip dysplasia and hypertrophic cardiomyopathy. No breeder can claim to have completely eradicated either from their line, but breeders do work hard to minimize the occurrence of these conditions.

A breeder who claims genetic issues have never surfaced in their cats isn't being honest. In my experience, however, when you see such problems with Maine Coon cats, they are more likely to be animals from backyard breeders or worse, from kitten mills.

Photo Credit: Johnnie Hardee of Megacoon Cattery

Please understand that I am not suggesting that backyard breeders are doing anything "bad." They have simply allowed their cat to have kittens and made those kittens available for adoption.

The problem is that there is no control over the genetics of the pairing. It is much more likely, under these circumstances, for a genetic flaw to be passed on.

I would never say don't adopt a Maine Coon cat from such a person, but I would strongly recommend that you have the kitten evaluated by a veterinarian first. Also ask a lot of questions about the parents and try to get a sense of their health. Meet them if possible.

Spaying or Neutering

The first medical procedure your pet will require is being spayed or neutered, as per the terms of the cattery's adoption agreement. (This is assuming you did acquire your cat from a recognized breeder.)

Catteries require written proof of the surgery before they will release the final registration papers. Costs vary, and there are options for having the procedure done for as little as $50 (£32.82).

Even though this is a substantial cost savings over the prices set at many clinics, I strongly suggest you find a vet in the beginning that will care for your Maine Coon in the long term. These surgeries are the real beginning of your pet's medical records, even though the baby will have likely received its initial vaccinations prior to adoption.

Spaying and neutering is usually performed before six months of age, although some breeders prefer to wait until the cat is 10-12 months of age, in order to give as much benefit as possible from the hormones on the bone and joint development.

If males are altered too late in life, or if the surgery is botched, damage to the urethra makes the cat subject to painful and life threatening bladder blockages.

Routine Health Care for Your Pet

In truth, you are the real foundation of your pet's health care program. Not only is it up to you to establish and maintain a working relationship with a qualified veterinarian, but you are also the one who will have the greatest sense of your cat's overall state of well-being, due to familiarity and daily association.

Clearly, in choosing a vet, you want a doctor with experience treating Maine Coons. I am also a huge advocate of the feline-only practices that have been growing in popularity for the past 25 years. The clinics are much quieter, which keeps the cats calmer, and the vets engage in ongoing continuing education in advances specifically related to the treatment of companion felines.

Interviewing a Veterinarian

Different cat owners like different styles in their interaction with veterinarians. I want a doctor with whom I can have a detailed discussion. Information is comforting to me, especially when I am anxious and unsure. My first instinct is to calm my fears with research. I want a vet who will meet me in that place.

At the same time, however, I want a vet who will talk to me and answer my questions honestly, no matter how much I may not like the answers. The animal in question is a member of my family, about whom I care very much. I have to know the truth in order to make good decisions on the cat's behalf.

A highly competent vet with a lousy bedside manner when interacting with *me* isn't someone I can work with. As for the cat? They aren't going to enjoy going to the vet, no matter what!

If you don't have a vet already, get a recommendation from the breeder, or look for local listings in the phone directory, or online.

Make an initial appointment for the express purpose of interviewing the vet. Be clear about that and about the fact that you are quite willing to pay for a regular visit. Vets are busy. Don't expect one to sit down and chat with you for nothing. Treat your vet like what he or she is: a medical professional.

Go in with prepared questions. Don't overstay your welcome. Get the information you need, including a basic list of costs for procedures. Only make an appointment to go in with your cat when you are satisfied that a clinic meets your needs and those of your pet.

At that time, observe closely how the vet and the technicians work with your pet. The desired demeanor should be efficient, calm, and firm. Don't interfere with their handling of your pet, unless asked. Vet techs know the best way to work with nervous, anxious cats.

Vaccinations

This will also be the point in your cat's life when you decide to continue with or forego vaccinations. This is, for many pet owners, a difficult choice. I can frankly see both sides of the debate.

Vaccinating companion animals against contagious disease has, without question, been a tremendous forward step in proper pet health care for decades. This is especially true in regard to legally mandated rabies shots.

Unfortunately, there is also credible evidence indicating vaccinations lead to the development of tumors at the site of the injection. This is a highly individual decision that I think any cat owner should only make after careful research and in consultation with a qualified veterinarian.

When you adopt a Maine Coon kitten from a cattery, the program of vaccinations will likely have already begun. You will have to decide whether or not you want to continue with the required boosters. The vaccinations typically given to cats include:

Combination Distemper

The combo for distemper, often referred to as FVRCP, is usually given at 8 weeks and again at 12 weeks, with a booster not due until 3 years later.

The intended protection includes:

- panleukopenia (FPV or feline infectious enteritis)

- rhinotracheitis (FVR, an upper respiratory /pulmonary infection)

- calicivirus (causes respiratory infections)

Some vaccines also guard against Chlamydophilia, which causes conjunctivitis.

Feline Leukemia

The leukemia vaccine is given to kittens at 2 months of age, followed by a booster a month or so later. Annual boosters are then given for life.

I cannot stress strongly enough that feline leukemia is so

infectious that it can be passed on by nothing more than a nose tap. You already know my belief that all cats, including Maine Coons, should be kept strictly indoors.

That being said, I do believe that the feline leukemia vaccine is essential for any cat that lives even part of the time outdoors. The risk of coming into contact with feral cats that are infected with the disease is simply too great.

Photo Credit: Johnnie Hardee of Megacoon Cattery

Rabies

Most local laws require that pet owners have their animals vaccinated against rabies and that proof of this compliance can be produced. Rabies injections typically cost around $40 (£26).

On-Going Preventive "Medicine"

The most important thing to understand about cats, in regard to ongoing preventive health care, is their instinctual urge to hide pain and signs of ill health. To put it bluntly, in the "real" world sick or injured animals are prey and vulnerable to attack by larger animals.

Owners must be even more vigilant about this instinct with a placid and calm breed like the Maine Coon. It is not at all unusual for a cat to be extremely ill before the owner realizes anything is wrong.

The Importance of Daily Handling

It always strikes me as odd to say, "all pets should be handled on a daily basis," since I can't keep my hands off mine, but touch and familiarity with the cat's habits and normal disposition are crucial to early detection of any abnormalities.

Never hold back from taking an animal to the vet for fear of seeming obsessive or overly concerned. No one knows your cat better than you do. If you sense that something is wrong, it probably is. Make an appointment!

Watch for all of the following signs of potential illness:

- Any change in weight or just the "feel" of your pet's body. Even through the thick coat of a Maine Coon, you should be able to feel the ribs just under a firm pad of healthy fat.

- Pay attention to how the cat moves and jumps. Is it getting around normally? Walking easily without a limp? Remember, Maine Coons are susceptible to hip dysplasia, so always pay attention to their ability to move well and without signs of discomfort.

- Look for signs of discharge from the nose or eyes. The problem could be nothing more than a respiratory infection from an allergy, but your vet still should evaluate the cat.

- Cats are very prone to infestations of ear mites. The irritation leads to scratching, which opens the door for more serious infection. Watch for ears that are hot and tender or that smell like yeast. Don't try to clean your cat's ears on your own. Make an appointment at the vet's.

- Watch for yellowed teeth, pale gums, red gums, and bad breath. These are signs of plaque build-up and periodontal disease. All cats can develop cancers of the mouth and throat. Regular dental exams are not only good for their teeth, but an opportunity to screen for lesions.

- Pay attention to how the cat is breathing. Normal respiration originates in the chest, not the belly.

- While grooming or petting, feel for the presence of any type of growth or mass. Even though many such growths are benign, they should all be evaluated immediately by your vet.

- Changes in normal litter box behavior can signal the presence of painful kidney or bladder infections, or even a life-threatening blockage. Don't assume an accident is an example of bad behavior. Go to the vet!

There have been enormous strides in the treatment of cats in the last two decades. Sadly, however, dog owners are still more likely to seek aggressive treatment for their pets. Don't ever make your cat a second-class citizen! Unless you are prepared to go the distance for your companion, rethink your desire to have a pet at all.

Worming

If you adopt a Maine Coon kitten from a reputable cattery, the chances of the baby having intestinal parasites or "worms" is slight. You'll know, however, if worms are present. You'll see them in the litter box.

If this does occur, take the cat to the vet for a full examination. Call in advance. You will likely be asked to bring a fresh stool sample.

Turn a clean plastic bag wrong side out and put your hand inside, as if the bag were a glove. Pick up the feces and fold the bag over the material, securing the bag shut. If you're a dog person, you'll recognize the maneuver from using "poop bags."

An oral deworming agent will be prescribed, with a second course of medication in 2-3 weeks, to ensure all eggs have been eradicated.

Hairballs

It always amuses me when a non-cat person asks, with genuine concern, "Oh my! Did your cat throw up a hairball?" I have to restrain myself from being a smart aleck and answering, "Did the sun come up today?"

It doesn't matter what kind of cat you have, or how long their fur might be. There always comes that moment, inevitably in the dark of the night when you've been sound asleep, that the hacking starts. In theory, cats can pass hairballs rather than regurgitate them, but in 40 years with felines, I've only had one that did that.

There's no mystery attached to hairballs. They are a natural consequence of self-grooming. The only time a hairball presents a health hazard is the rare instances of a blockage, signaled by the cat's refusal to eat. If the vet takes an X-ray and finds a hairball is blocking the digestive tract, surgery may be required. Clearly the best way to help your cat with the matter of hairballs is just to brush the cat!

Potential Genetic Conditions in Maine Coons

All of my Maine Coons have been very healthy cats, but the breed is associated with two genetic conditions: hip dysplasia and hypertrophic cardiomyopathy.

Hip Dysplasia

Hip dysplasia is caused by a defective hip socket, which causes the cat to move slowly and to be very reluctant to jump or climb. It can be quite severe, hampering movement and causing great pain, or be nothing more than a mild annoyance.

There is no way to guarantee that hip dysplasia will not be present in a line of Maine Coons and no breeder should ever make this claim. These are seriously big cats anyway, so it's very important that they not be allowed to become obese, which will exacerbate the chances of hip dysplasia presenting in an otherwise healthy animal.

Depending on the severity of the condition, it can either be
controlled with pain medication or corrective surgery may be
needed.

Many people equate the hip problems associated with large dogs
to large cats, but cats move differently and are more flexible.
Many stories have circulated about a cat diagnosed with hip
dysplasia by X-ray and yet that same cat is still able to jump to
the top of a refrigerator. It just isn't as big of a quality of life issue
with cats as it can be with dogs.

Hypertrophic Cardiomyopathy

Virtually any breed of cat can develop hypertrophic
cardiomyopathy (HCM). The illness causes the heart muscle to
thicken, reducing its capacity to function. HCM can only be
detected with an echocardiogram.

As HCM progresses, fluid accumulates in the lungs and blood
clots form. Eventually the animal will die of heart failure. There
is no cure for HCM.

Sharon Stegall of Dracoonfly Maine Coon Cattery is a breeder
who screens her breeding cats' hearts by ultrasound. She says:
"Maine Coon cats are certainly not the only cat to be subject to
heart disease, but since we were the first breed that became part
of a research project studying the heritability of HCM in cats, we
are often associated with the disease.

HCM affects many cats, pedigreed and not. It does seem to be
hereditary, which is why responsible cat breeders will have the
hearts of their breeding cats echoed on a regular basis (one echo
at a year of age isn't enough) to try to eliminate the disease from
their lines.

A DNA test came out in 2005 which identifies one of the mutations (called cMyBP-C) responsible for HCM in the Maine Coon. It's a nice predictor — however; a cat which tests negative can still get HCM from unknown factors or other genetic mutations which don't have a reliable test yet. Therefore, ultrasound performed by a board certified cardiologist familiar with Maine Coons is still the best screening device we have.

Better yet is getting a kitten not only from recently echoed parents, but who also has several screened cats behind its pedigree. Still, it's no guarantee, as heart disease is complicated. While HCM in an older cat isn't desirable, many factors play into the health of a geriatric feline (like diet and obesity) so we focus on HCM in the young cats."

As Your Pet Ages

Like all cats, Maine Coons age in some fairly predictable ways as they experience changes in their senses and physical abilities. You shouldn't expect any two cats to grow old the same way, but there are obvious signs of aging. Some cats remain quite spry to the end, however, and this has been my experience with the Maine Coon.

Decreased Senses

Like humans, older cats lose their ability to see, hear, smell, and taste with the same acuity they enjoyed early in life. The changes may never be apparent to you. Cats cope extremely well.

The same elderly Himalayan I inherited went completely blind. I never knew anything was wrong until I rearranged the living room furniture and the cat started banging into chair legs.

I took her to the vet and was shocked to discover her vision was gone. In her case, the culprit was cataracts, but high blood pressure often causes blindness in elderly felines.

You may notice that older cats get thinner as their appetites diminish. This is actually tied to a decrease in their ability to smell their food, so it may be necessary to tempt a senior cat with more aromatic supper choices.

This tactic can be a two-edged sword, however. Rich foods also cause gastrointestinal upset. I opt to dribble a little fresh tuna or sardine juice on my older cats' food when they seem disinterested in eating.

This adds just enough scent to get them interested in their chow again. You can also try warming wet food just slightly to enhance the odor. If these tactics don't work, consult with your vet about safe appetite stimulants.

Physical Changes

In addition to potential changes in eating habits, older cats are leaner because they have less muscle mass. This is harder to see through a Maine Coon's thick coat. Be sure to feel your pet's body conformation regularly. If you can feel the animal's ribs, a vet should examine the cat. Excessive weight loss is dangerous in senior cats.

Pay attention to how your cat's coat looks and help him out if he seems to need extra grooming. This includes the more "personal" areas, since arthritis may make squatting in the litter box more difficult. It's sometimes necessary to shave a longhaired cat's hindquarters to prevent soiling.

If you do have to clean your cat's "private" areas, do so with a warm washcloth and plain, clean water.

Personality Changes

Subtle changes in personality and behavior can indicate sickness or even unhappiness. If a cat with arthritis can no longer reach his favorite spot to sun, that fact can depress him in the way a former athlete might look longingly at younger players on the field. Help your cat with a ramp or "stairs" so he can continue to live his life as normally as possible.

Although neither lazy nor lethargic, Maine Coons are mellow cats. As they age, they'll sleep for longer periods, which is just a reflection of naturally slowing down. So long as your pet is eating well, this change in behavior isn't necessarily a symptom of actual illness.

Senior cats should have regular checkups and should see the vet any time you feel uneasy about their behavior and overall demeanor. Extra vigilance is always called for, but use your judgment and your own intimate knowledge of your cat's personality and way of being in the world.

End of Life Decisions

Emotional strength is a major part of responsible pet ownership when end of life decisions are required. I have had to do this many times and always with a heavy heart, no matter how sure I was that the decision was correct. I would never presume to tell you or anyone else when it is "time." I will suggest some things, however, that might help you to make the decision.

First, take the advice of your veterinarian. I trust my vet implicitly. She knows my cats and she knows me. She doesn't lie to me or give me false hope, but she also knows that I will do whatever is necessary to support my pets' lives until they tell me it's time to go.

Yes, to a non-cat person that may sound absurd, but if I have a cat that is clearly enjoying its life, but requires a treatment or a medication, euthanasia is never on the table. And no, it has not always been the wisest financial choice.

I know my cats. I know when they are in pain and not enjoying a good quality of life. I do not believe that I have ever been responsible for causing an animal to suffer by "waiting too long." They tell me when they are done and ready to move on. I honor their wishes.

If you have not had the experience of being with a pet in those last moments, please believe what I am about to tell you. With the assistance of a kind and professional veterinarian, the process is completely dignified, fast, and painless.

In every instance, my pet and I have been afforded the privacy and calm of a quiet room. I have always been given ample time to say good-bye and to hold and comfort the cat as the injection is administered.

Nothing I say can stop your pain or assuage your grief, but I hope that the knowledge that your pet will not suffer, and will be treated with respect, gives you some comfort when the time comes.

I also want to say that absolutely no one should ever sit in judgment on the decisions you make on behalf of your pet. I have spent large amounts of money on treatments for my cats, but I did not have family obligations that prevented me from doing so.

Whatever factors influence your decision, so long as you are motivated by kindness and a sincere desire to make the best choice for your pet that you can, in the larger context of your life, no one can ask more of you.

Chapter 8 - Cat Shows and Breeding Explained

These two topics are being put in the same chapter because most people who breed Maine Coon cats either exhibit them or are regular attendees at cat shows.

I'm in the latter category. I don't show my cats, but I have attended many, many cat shows. As obvious as it may sound to say so, if you've never been to one, it's not a dog show.

At one time or another almost everyone has been flipping through the channels and watched a few minutes of the annual Westminster Dog Show. What you see there in no way correlates with exhibiting a cat.

Photo Credit: Robin Warren of Red Flannel Cattery

Here's the major difference: dogs *like* dog shows. Cats, on their very best day and in their best mood, *tolerate* the experience.

Maine Coons are a very cooperative breed and show well, but

this fact doesn't alter the major differences in how cats are shown as opposed to dogs.

Dogs are rarely crated at shows and happily walk around on their leads or lie patiently at their owner's feet. You'll also see show dogs being groomed and fluffed up without complaint.

Cats are crated *all the time*. They'll stage a jailbreak in an instant, as evidenced by the dreaded cry of "loose cat!" Show cats may be forced to endure being combed and groomed before going into the ring, but they clearly are not having the time of their lives.

How Cat Shows Work

For all these differences, and for the cats' minimal agreement with the nonsense, a cat show is a festive affair. Since the animals are only removed from their cages for judging, exhibitors go all-out decorating their assigned area.

Attendees stroll up and down admiring both the cats and the displays. Everything seems calm and pleasant, but there's always a frantic undercurrent. Long periods of boredom are punctuated by mad dashes to the ring.

You will find vendors for all-things-feline taking advantage of the slow pace. It's extremely easy to spend a lot of money at cat shows, but it's not an adoption venue or even a place to negotiate a potential purchase.

Entrants are judged according to formalized breed standards drawn up by the governing body for the show. Each organization may have slightly different rules, but the show standards are essentially uniform.

The major organizations in the cat fancy are:

- American Association of Cat Enthusiasts
- American Cat Fanciers Association
- The International Cat Association
- Fédération Internationale Féline
- World Cat Federation
- Cat Fanciers Association
- Feline Federation Europe
- Australia Cat Federation

Understanding the Cat Show Atmosphere

There's one huge rule at cat shows. Don't touch. Yes, it's frustrating, but it's entirely for the protection of the cats. If you were to touch a cat suffering from an illness, and then touched a second animal, your hands could be the vectors for transmitting the illness.

If you are invited to pet one of the cats, you are being paid a supreme compliment, one delivered with a bottle of hand sanitizer. Don't be offended. Just use it. Remember, you're protecting the cat, not your own ego.

Also, never try to help in instances when a cat escapes. Just freeze in place. If you see the animal, quietly indicate its presence, but don't try to catch the runaway. You'll only add to the confusion and scare the cat more.

Stay out of the way at all times. It's quite common for a competitor rushing to the show ring to yell, "Right of way!" When you hear that, move! Exhibitors only have a brief amount of time to get to the judging area or face disqualification. Keep your eyes and ears open and learn from what's going on around you. You can gain a great deal of information on individual breeds by listening to the comments the judges make as they are evaluating each animal.

The Maine Coon Breed Group Show Standard

Judging in cat shows is a complicated business requiring judges to learn intricate breed standards. The actual awarding of ribbons and trophies is based on the simple fact that the cats that most closely conform to the ideal standard receive the highest marks.

Ranking the cats, however, takes an experienced and practiced eye. To give you an idea of the difficulty of this process, I've reproduced The International Cat Association Maine Coon Breed Group Show standard verbatim below.

HEAD - 40 points

Shape - 8
Eyes - 5
Ears - 10
Muzzle and Chin - 10
Profile - 7

BODY - 35 points

Torso - 10
Legs and Feet - 3
Tail - 5
Boning - 7
Musculature - 10

COAT/COLOR/PATTERN - 25 points

Length - 10
Texture - 5
Color - 5
Pattern - 5

CATEGORY - Traditional
DIVISIONS - All
COLORS - All
PERMISSIBLE OUTCROSSES: None

Overall balance and proportion are essential to the Maine Coon and no one feature should dominate the eye's attention over any other.

HEAD - Shape

Broad, modified wedge. Size in proportion to body. Slightly longer than wide. Distinct muzzle break can be seen under high prominent cheekbones.

Eyes - Large, slightly oval, appear round when wide open. Outer corner of eye points toward outer base of ear. Wide-set.

Color: Any shade of green and/or gold. No relationship to coat color. Blue and odd-eyes accepted in whites and particolors.

Ears - Large, wide at base with outer base set just slightly farther back than inner base. Outer base just above the level of the top of the eye. Outside edges have a very slight outward tilt that is not past eleven and one o'clock. Set fairly high on head with inner edge of ear bases no more than one ear's width apart. Taller than the width at base but still in balance with head length. Moderately pointed ears appear taller due to lynx tips. Furnishings extend beyond outer edge of ear.

Chin - Wide and deep enough to complete square look of muzzle. Firm, in line with upper lip.

Muzzle - Square

Profile - Gently curving forehead. Gentle concave curve at bridge of nose flowing into a smooth nose line. Slight nose bump allowed in kittens.

BODY - Torso

Large, long, substantial, rectangular, equal in breadth from shoulders to hips. Broad chest. Level back. Females may be noticeably smaller than males.

Legs - Medium length to form a rectangle with the body.

Feet - Large, round, and well-tufted.

Tail – At least as long as the body. Wide at base and tapering to a tip with full, flowing fur.

Boning – Substantial

Musculature – Substantial, powerful.

COAT - Length

Uneven; shorter on shoulders, gradually lengthening down the back and sides. Long, full, shaggy belly fur, and britches. Tail fur long, full, flowing. Frontal ruff becomes more developed with age.

Texture - All weather coat. A slight undercoat gives the coat body but coat still falls smoothly. Not cottony.

Color : Particolors must have some white on all four feet.

GENERAL DESCRIPTION

The Maine Coon is America's native longhaired cat. The breed, with its essentially amiable disposition, developed through a natural selection process where only the fittest survived. It should always be remembered that the Maine Coon developed basically as a "working cat" able to fend for itself in rough, woody terrain and under extreme climatic conditions. The Maine Coon is a large breed with big ears, broad chest, substantial boning, a long, hard muscled, rectangular body, and a long flowing tail. Good muscle tone and density give the cat the appearance of power.

ALLOWANCES

Standard favors the male. Allowance MUST be made for a significant size difference between the male and the female. Type should not be sacrificed for size. Breed is slow to mature. Allow for tighter earset in kittens and wider earset in mature adults.

PENALIZE:

Eye - Slanted, almond-shaped. Flat tops on openings.

Ears - Very close, set straight up. Narrow bases. Wide set, flared.

Chin - Weak or receding, narrow, lack of depth.

Muzzle - Prominent whisker pads.

Profile - Straight. Roman nose. Pronounced bump.

Torso - Narrow

Tail - Short tail

Coat - Lack of slight undercoat or belly shag. Overall even coat.

Color - Obvious lockets.

Considering Becoming a Breeder?

There are entire books devoted to the mechanics of becoming a professional cat breeder. That discussion isn't my purpose here, but I do have a few observations I'd like to share.

When I sit down with a prospective breeder, I have to smother a laugh when they tell me they expect to open a cattery as a profitable business.

Yes, purebred Maine Coon kittens, or any other breed for that matter, command high prices. But please believe me when I tell you that the money goes out just as quickly as it comes in.

There is only one reason to become a breeder of pedigreed cats — love of the breed and a desire to cultivate a genetic line that showcases it to its ultimate perfection.

The questions you should be asking yourself have less to do with money and more to do with commitment.

Breeding cats is not a 9 to 5 job. You will be giving up nights, weekends, vacations, and holidays, especially if you cannot afford a support staff. The cats will be in charge of your schedule and the unexpected happens constantly.

Can You Deal With the Pains?

There are far more pains than you realize. No matter how confident I am that a kitten is going to a good home, the good-byes are devastating. I want to keep them all!

There are the babies that don't make it because they are born too small or contract an infection they're too young to fight off. If you raise cats, you will lose cats. If you can't even stand the thought of that heartbreak, you shouldn't be a cat breeder.

Can You Pay For It?

The expense doesn't just involve equipment, but also the foundation animals for your line, or the stud fees if you can't afford to buy a breeding pair.

Put equipment, food, supplies, and vet expenses on the list. You may even have to add on to your home and put a liability rider on your homeowner's insurance policy.

For all the expenses for which you carefully prepare, there will be two dozen more that blindside you.

What Will the Neighbors Think?

Maine Coon cats are very quiet. Noise isn't the issue, but have you considered if the area in which you live is zoned for running a home business?

Are you a member of a homeowner's association? What are the HOA rules and regulations about home businesses? Number of pets? What permits and licenses will you require? What will you have to do to pass health inspections? Is parking an issue?

This is a list that can, and should be, long and comprehensive to the point of absurdity. You have to live in your home and neighbor "wars" are miserable. Get all details of this sort worked out before you bring innocent cats into the fray.

Also, what are the requirements in your state and what guarantees are you required to offer?

Some states require you to pay the kitten's vet bills if the new owner has any problems during the first year.

Some states require yearly inspections by the Department of Agriculture.

US states vary a great deal in requirements for breeders. It's the breeder's responsibility to know local law.

What Will You Do if You Fail?

I'm an optimist. I never start anything with the expectation of failure. However, when you start a cattery, it isn't your welfare on the line. You are responsible for the wellbeing of your cats.

If you fail, can you keep them all? If not, where will they go? Never contemplate breeding cats if you don't have an exit strategy that is focused entirely on their needs.

Summary Thoughts

Now, granted, I've sounded pretty negative for the last couple of pages. What I've been trying to do is explain things to you realistically.

If you immerse yourself in the cat fancy, learn everything there is to know about a breeding operation, do all your financial due diligence, and still decide to move forward? You're in for a rewarding, consuming, and thoroughly satisfying life experience.

The only gold standard for your decision-making should be: what is right for the cats? You can make your own choices. They can only deal with the circumstances in which you place them. Never forget that.

Afterword

My love for Maine Coons goes well beyond their pleasingly solid bulk and vaguely wild appearance. Yes, my heart goes pitter patter at the sight of those tufted ears and high cheekbones. But what I really love is the gentleness, intelligence, and companionable nature of these cats.

I've lived with cats all my life, and I proudly wear the mantle of "crazy cat lady." I love to watch and interact with cats, and I try, in so much as I can, to understand their way of being in the world.

As much as I know it's not necessarily the "right" thing to do, I am guilty of anthropomorphizing my animals — assigning human qualities to them. So with that disclaimer, the Maine Coon is the kind of cat you can have a beer with and tell all your troubles to!

He's a buddy, a pal, the friend who will always know when to make you laugh and when to commiserate and hand you a tissue. You've never really had a cat for a chum until you've lived your life with a Maine Coon.

I can't say the breed has spoiled me for all other kinds of cats, but they're certainly high on my list. I realize, in the writing of this book, I've often referred to Maine Coons as "he." Typically I do have male cats and with this breed, I especially like the boys because they're so big.

A Maine Coon is just a thoroughly satisfying cat to have in your life, both in terms of temperament and physical bulk. They're smart, good-humored, hardy, and long lived.

As I said in the foreword, pretty much the ideal cat, in my book.

If these are qualities that appeal to you as well, I can truthfully say you won't go wrong with a Maine Coon. They are excellent cats and outstanding pets.

Photo Credit: Image © Sarah Beth Photography – Supplied by Rock Hill Maine Coons

Frequently Asked Questions

While I strongly suggest that you read the entire text of this book to truly appreciate the Maine Coon breed, and to understand the proper husbandry these beautiful cats require, the following are some of the most frequently asked questions about Maine Coon cats as pets.

What should I look for in selecting a Maine Coon kitten?

Kittens should not be offered for adoption before 12 weeks of age. The babies should be happily interested in the world around them, exhibiting only a little initial shyness. Their eyes, nose, and ears should all be clean and free of any discharge.

Look for fur that is soft, shiny, and completely intact with no bald patches. A kitten's body should feel solid and healthy, not bony. Ask the breeder to gently pull back the baby's lips so you can see the gums, which should be pink and healthy looking.

What's the best way to find a good breeder?

I personally think that the best way to find a really good breeder is to attend cat shows. There, you can see the finest animals a cattery has to exhibit. While this is not a venue in which you can adopt a cat, it's a great place to look at cats and to meet breeders.

Are Maine Coon kittens born with long hair?

I'd describe Maine Coon babies as little fluff balls. They certainly come into the world with denser hair than other breeds. The Maine Coon is a slow maturing breed, so the full coat won't come in until around age 3 anyway.

Do Maine Coon cats require any kind of special diet?

While it is certainly possible for a Maine Coon, or any other cat, to require a special diet due to some sort of health condition, the vast majority thrive on the same kind of balanced and varied died that is appropriate for any companion feline.

How much grooming is required for a Maine Coon?

Although Maine Coons have thick coats, their fur is silky and weather resistant. It doesn't tangle as easily as that of other longhaired breeds. A 5-15 minute combing and brushing, three or more times per week, with a trip to the groomer's every 3 months or so, should be sufficient.

What equipment is needed for grooming?

The best implement for the Maine Coon coat is a metal comb with alternating short and long teeth. Brushes can be used, but since they may contribute to, rather than solve, tangling and matting, only purchase a brush after consulting with your breeder or with a professional groomer.

At what age should I begin to groom my Maine Coon daily?

The sooner a cat becomes familiar and comfortable with a grooming routine, the better. If you buy your Maine Coon from a reputable breeder, the baby will come to you already accustomed to being combed. Discuss the cat's existing routine with the breeder, and replicate that schedule exactly.

Also, it's always a good idea to begin and end a grooming session by concentrating on an area that feels extra good for kitty, like just below the chin. You always want your cat to associate grooming with a pleasant experience.

Will my Maine Coon shed more during certain seasons?

All cats, including longhaired cats like the Maine Coon, shed more in the warmer months of the year. Starting in the spring and carrying through the summer, you will likely have to increase combing sessions and perhaps even tend your cat's coat daily.

Is there any difference in temperament and adaptability in a male or female Maine Coon?

While the gender question is a standard one, it isn't a question that I regard as necessarily fair or accurate. All cats, regardless of gender, are individuals. They all have distinct personalities, and they all respond to their life experiences.

I have had many cats of all species and both genders, including Maine Coons. They are all lovely, well-mannered, sweet pets and I see no apparent difference in personality between the genders.

Is there a problem with male Maine Coon cats spraying?

Spraying can happen with a male cat of any breed, but it is not an issue with which I've ever had to deal, even with my intact males.

In neutered males, spraying is highly unlikely for the simple reason that they are typically altered within the first six months of life. At that age, they're too young to have even contemplated the spraying behavior.

Many people do not realize that female cats can spray too, but again, this is extremely rare behavior. In my experience, cats that are happy, healthy, and well cared for just don't spray. This is a stereotype that is unfairly applied to toms, and in my experience, indicative of an unhappy or physically ill cat.

If spraying does occur, it is much more typical in a multi-cat household where issues of territoriality arise. Again, however, this is not an issue I've faced with my cats, even when I've had 25 and more at one time.

What is Polydactylism?

The issue of polydactylism ("mitten pawed", "double-thumbed", "snowshoe pawed") comes up often with Maine Coons. The breed was originally bred to keep the rodent population down on damp, cold New England fishing vessels. Extra digits, usually extra thumbs, may have developed over the decades to help cats maneuver in Maine's deep snow.

Maine Coons were one of the original breeds to be shown in US cat shows. The first known cat show was at the Crystal Palace in Chicago, 1890 — Maine Coons were shown and polydactyls were quite common.

By the 1920s, the exotic breeds had become popular, and Maine Coons fell out of favor. For a few decades, they were actually not a recognized breed for show purposes.

When Maine Coon breeders wanted to re-introduce the breed into the show arena in the 1950s, they were afraid that any weird or disfiguring characteristic would make it harder for the breed to be accepted, so polydactylism was gradually bred out of the show breed. The show registries such as CFA and TICA required non-polydactylism as part of the breed standard.

Now that the breed is very accepted in the shows, breeders are trying to reintroduce polydactylism as a normal Maine Coon trait. TICA now allows poly Maine Coons to be shown in the New Traits class.

Bonus Chapter 1 - Breed Expert Sharon Stegall

Sharon, thanks for doing this interview, can you tell us who you are and where you are based?

I live with my family in Connecticut. My registered cattery name is Dracoonfly, like dragonfly with a "coon" in the middle.

Just how did your interest in Maine Coons start?

I've always had cats; two shelter kitties, no more, no less (which is hard to believe now). Like many Maine Coon breeders, I had a "Maine Coon Wannabee." I had her when I was in college at UNC-Chapel Hill. She was just a pretty Domestic Longhair, but because of Felicity, I became aware of the breed.

Years later, I decided I wanted to get a third cat who was closer in age to my youngest Domestic Short Hair. I now had the money to get what I really wanted, a Maine Coon, so I purchased my first pedigreed cat, Sassy.

What can a new owner expect in terms of differences between this breed and others?

Size, beauty, and a strange, squeaky meow that doesn't fit the stature of the cat. Men in particular love Maine Coons because their size is so formidable and manly.

How did you progress from owner to becoming a top breeder?

I decided before-hand that if I was going to breed Maine Coons, it would only be with the goal of improving the breed. This meant committing to cat shows to establish the quality of my breeding cats and screening my breeding cats to ensure healthy kittens. With this in mind, I set out to buy my first Maine Coon, Sassy, with breeding rights.

Without breeding rights, you can't register any resulting kittens and, in essence, become a backyard breeder. Because I showed, when it came time to choose a mate for Sassy, I knew several breeders who now trusted me and were willing to let me use their stud.

Most breeders are very picky about to whom they will offer stud service. After a couple of years, I was able to find my own male to use for breeding. He and Sassy produced a national winning kitten.

However, I'm convinced that the major reason I'm known among kitten buyers is because I maintain an updated website and Facebook page and I write a blog, Sharon Space, which tries to educate cat owners (and covers other subjects as well).

Now you also show your cats, how did it start for you?

I've always shown, starting with my first Maine Coon, Sassy, at 4 months old. She did well and I became obsessed with showing. I did not start out the way that's recommended for new breeders, which would be showing a neutered male Maine Coon in order to learn more about the breed and to network.

Can you offer any advice to others who may be wondering if they can also start showing?

For owners of pet Maine Coons, I would first turn to the breeder you bought your cat from and ask if your cat would be considered show quality and if your breeder would be willing to mentor you.

It is far easier to start showing with a kitten than to expect an older cat to accept the demands of a cat show. A cat has to be bathed, dried, and travel to a large venue where other cats, strangers, and a public address system can be very stressful to the non-indoctrinated cat.

A mentor is essential to teach a novice about showing. CFA and TICA offer mentor programs if the kitten's breeder is unable to help. And yes, cats can be shown if they are neutered or spayed; it's a separate category from the intact cats, called Premiership in CFA and the Alter class in TICA.

I should also mention that many cat shows offer a separate class for the non-pedigreed cats, called Household Pets, in order to encourage owners of "moggies" to get involved.

Can you offer advice to people looking to buy a Maine Coon?

The most important thing is to find a good, responsible breeder who stands behind his/her kittens' health.

A breeder should be willing to provide proof that the parents of the kittens have had their hearts screened, utilizing ultrasound or echo-cardiogram (same thing).

Do not expect the kittens themselves to have been echoed. If HCM were to show up, it normally wouldn't be detectable until a cat is past the age of two years. There is a DNA test which identifies one of the mutations (called cMyBP-C) that causes hypertrophic cardiomyopathy (HCM) in the Maine Coon, but unfortunately, HCM isn't that simple. Therefore, the best test for healthy hearts continues to be ultrasound.

With most of my breeding cats, I can demonstrate that not only has the cat itself been screened, but so have its parents, grandparents, great-grandparents, maybe even a couple of aunts, uncles, siblings, and offspring.

There can be other health issues breeders have tested, such as hip dysplasia, Spinal Muscular Atrophy (SMA), and Pyruvate Kinase Deficiency, but those issues are much rarer than heart disease.

In finding the right kitten from the right breeder, remember that Maine Coons are a very popular breed so a good breeder's kittens go quickly. Here in the States, there are more breeders located on the East and West Coasts.

Location and how far someone is willing to travel will determine not only price, but how available kittens are for a prospective buyer.

In Europe, there are many more Maine Coon breeders than there are in the U.S. A prospective kitten buyer should not expect to call a breeder and drop by to shop. We are busy and our cats are part of our home; not a store front.

Contact several breeders to discover when kittens are expected, if there is a waiting list involved, etc. I personally prefer to be contacted initially by email so I can answer questions when it's convenient. Otherwise, I'd spend too much of my day on the phone.

Are there things that you see owners doing that frustrate you?

Most of the owners of my kittens/cats are wonderful people, so my pet peeves are minimal. Not keeping up with clipping claws or grooming can be a reoccurring issue with some.

Another is allowing the cat to become too fat and feeding inferior grade cat food. A cat should not weigh over 30 pounds just because it is a Maine Coon!

Do you have any tips for new owners of a kitten?

All new kittens should start out in a room and not allowed to have full access to the house until he/she is comfortable. If a home has multiple levels, there should be a litter box on each floor as kittens have short-term memories and get distracted easily, like a small child. The litter box can be moved to the basement if desired after the kitten is about 6-months-old.

What feeding routines and types of food/supplements do you

recommend?

I free-feed a high protein dry food and feed canned food twice daily. There are many good brands, but I think it's better to avoid dry food that has corn meal listed in the first five ingredients. If a cat is becoming too heavy, I recommend restricting the amount of dry food, as it contains so many carbohydrates, and substituting more canned food.

Are there accessories that you can particularly recommend?

Litter boxes and carriers need to take into account that a full-grown Maine Coon is larger than normal. Scratching posts, a steel-tooth comb, and nail clippers should be standard supplies in any cat home.

Sharon, thanks for helping our readers with your expert advice.
Sharon Stegall of Dracoonfly Maine Coon Cattery
http://www.dracoonfly.com
http://dracoonfly.blogspot.co.uk/

Bonus Chapter 2 - Breed Expert Terrie Lyons

Terrie, thanks for doing this interview. Can you tell us who you are and where you are based?

I am Terrie Lyons. I live in a hamlet called Budletts, just outside the town of Uckfield, in East Sussex, United Kingdom.

Terrie with husband Barry

Just how did your interest in Maine Coons start?

I wanted to have cats when I moved here nearly 18 years ago, but was warned by the electrician, working on our house, not to let them out, as the country road at the bottom of our road was a killer of cats. So I set up making a safe area for them before buying one. I went to a cat show and fell in love with the Maine Coon. I bought my first female a little later.

What differences might new owners notice, compared to other types of cat?

The main difference, excuse the pun, is the size. The female is bigger than most other cats and the male can be enormous. Both sexes are very affectionate and friendly and laid back, which is not the case in all other breeds.

They can be very dog like and love playing ball. They can even be trained to do cat agility. This is done with a lure, and not tidbits, as with dogs.

Can you offer any advice to people looking to buy a Maine Coon, where to buy, what to look out for, etc.?

When people contact me regarding purchasing a Maine Coon, and I haven't got kittens at that time, I advise that they stick to registered breeders on the Maine Coon cat club website and put their name on the waiting list.

Kittens are very sought-after, some of mine are reserved before they are born. People are encouraged to come and meet my cats in the fur, having seen them on my website.

I also advise against buying a kitten from someone that works full time. The kitten will not be well socialized and possibly not kept too clean.

I recommend seeing both parents of the new kitten. Temperament does breed through genetically and if either parent is bad tempered or unfriendly it is not advisable to purchase said kitten. It could be alright, but it is not worth taking the risk.

Also ask if all the breeder's cats are vaccinated every year. Some breeders don't do this.

Are there things that you see owners doing that frustrate you?

It is very frustrating when they ignore advice and the kitten has an accident or the food is changed and the kitten gets an upset tummy. Recently one of my new owners had a sick cat and the vets were puzzled. It turned out after an X-ray that the cat had eaten two twenty pence coins.

Another danger is plants and flowers. Another is busy roads.

How should new owners approach bringing a new kitten home? Any advice or tips you can give?

Taking a new kitten home can be traumatic for the 3 month old Maine Coon. I suggest that the first thing the new owner does is use one room to start with. The whole house could be very daunting.

In that one room the litter tray should be ready to receive the kitten and I tell the new owners to take the kitten out of the carrier and put it in the litter tray to climb out on its own. That way it knows where the bathroom is.

A little portion of a kitten pouch will help the new owner bond with the kitten. Play with the kitten with a ball, laser pen, or similar. Pick the kitten up for cuddles and it can be taken to another room to watch TV, etc., but put it back in the one room for the night.

Usually the kitten can have the run of the whole home very quickly. It is advisable though, if they are allowed upstairs, to put another litter tray on the landing or bathroom. Remember the kitten is a baby and might suddenly want to use a tray.

What feeding routines and types of food/supplements do you recommend?

I use a top quality food specially made for the breed (Royal Canin). The Maine Coon is a very slow maturing cat and is not fully grown until 4 years of age. You keep them on the Maine Coon kitten food until 15 months old, which is much longer than any other cat. You then transfer to the adult food.

I also use their 'Intense Hairball' which I mix in to assist with the furball problem. It is a complete food and can be safely left out for the cat to graze. Soft food can be used as a treat, but it is not necessary to feed it. The Royal Canin has all the minerals, vitamins, and supplements that the cat requires. I use filtered water for my cats (I have a fridge that filters it) so I recommend that people change over to tap water slowly.

Are there accessories that you can particularly recommend for owners to buy?

Maine Coons love heights and will learn to climb very early. Before they leave here, they are already at the top of the climbing towers.

It is essential that they have a substantial scratching post, and if buying a tower, that it is made for the heavier cat. It might be a good idea to secure it to a wall. If it fell over the cat could be killed.

Maine Coons can also be a bit clumsy and I recommend putting away ornaments, etc., for a while.

A laser pen is a wonderful toy for the kitten and good exercise. They will happily chase it for quite some time. Just avoid the face.

If you buy toys on a string, do not leave it out, they can swallow the string which could cause an obstruction and the cat would need it to be surgically removed. Ping pong balls are a favorite toy and many bring it back in their mouths to be thrown again.

I recommend giant litter trays, covered, but take the flap off. I also recommend a good cat litter, i.e. The World's Best Cat Litter or similar. Town dwellers can put this safely down the toilet. People living in major towns would find this beneficial.

I also recommend going online for wormers and flea preparations, which are much cheaper than the vets.

Do you have any special grooming tips?

I recommend that as soon as the kitten is settled that they are groomed for a few minutes a day, to get them used to it. Especially the trousers, as I call them, when they get older. This is a part they don't like being groomed. Under the arms and the belly is good to be done.

At this young age, the kitten will happily turn on its back to have its belly groomed. I also show people how to "pop claws" which is a gentle pressing on the top of the toe so that the claw pops out. If people do this from a young age, the cat will not object when it is older.

You don't cut the claws immediately, you wait until the kitten is comfortable with the claw popping and then just take the tips off. Young children should be well covered when cuddling the kitten, they could be scratched by the very sharp little claws. They learn as they get older to keep their claws retracted.

Thanks so much, Terrie, for sharing your expertise.

Mrs Terrie Lyons of Budletts Maine Coons
http://www.mainecoonkittens.me.uk

Bonus Chapter 3 - Taking Your Kitten Home

Robin Warren of Red Flannel Cattery has kindly agreed to let us reprint her manual she gives to new owners.

The information in this document is provided as a service, and is based purely on our experience in the cattery. No qualifications for giving medical, dietary, or behavioral advice are implied. Red Flannel Cattery is not liable for injury or damage resulting from the advice given here. Always rely on your veterinarian for all medical, dietary, and behavioral advice.

Before You Pick Up Your Kitten

Your breeder may require you to have your veterinarian confirm the health of your kitten within a short period of time. If necessary, make an appointment with your vet.

Acquire the following minimum supplies:

- Cat Carrier - We recommend those that allow loading from the top as well as the end. Soft-sided and fabric carriers are not strong enough for an adult Maine Coon.

- Food Dishes - Dishes should be made of glass, metal, or glazed pottery.

- Food and Litter - For both, use the brand recommended by your breeder.

- Litter Box. Your kitten will probably be fully prepared to use a full-sized litter box, but check with your breeder. If you need a smaller one for a short time, a dishpan-sized box will do fine.

Room Set-Up

Your new kitten will be bombarded with new smells, sounds, and people, and can easily be frightened. He needs to become accustomed to his new environment in a place where he feels totally safe and secure. Restrict your kitten to a single room until he has relaxed, learned the ropes, and bonded with you. An office, bathroom, walk-in closet, or laundry room would be fine. (Bedrooms, if he can hide deep under the bed, are not advised.) The room should be off limits to children and to other household pets, and should be quiet. Food, water, and kitty litter should be readily accessible. Give your kitten a soft place to sleep, preferably elevated. Be sure there is a cozy place in the room where your new kitten can hide — the cat carrier works perfectly.

Please do not let your kitten sleep with you in the bedroom unless you are absolutely sure that you will allow this forever. Once your kitten sleeps with you, he will never want to sleep anywhere else.

Gradually, as his confidence with you grows, your kitten will explore his new home. But he will feel safer in a small area at first. But we recommend that your kitten stay in the safe room overnight for the first night or two, or perhaps longer if there are children or other pets. He may be lonely when he's alone, but that is ok. This will make him much more affectionate when you arrive.

Kitten Stress

Think we're kidding? Stress in young (and adult) cats is very real. A stressed kitten is more likely to get sick, vomit, get diarrhea, scratch you, make litter mistakes, hide, cry, or begin bad habits. So you will want to minimize stressors to your kitten whenever possible.

Here are some things that cause stress in kittens:

• Going home with a new owner, or moving to a new house.

• Changing the daily ritual.

• Introducing a new animal to the household.

• Getting shots or going to the vet.

• Changing food, or changing its location.

• Switching to a new brand of kitty litter, or moving the litter box.

• Situations that are frightening to a kitten.

Try to avoid doing too many of these things at once.

When You Get Home

Introduce your kitten to the safe room first. Take the carrier into the room, open the carrier, and leave. Give him plenty of time to explore it — he is looking for hidden dangers and for hiding places.

Your kitten will be lonely and cry for you once he has explored his new space. Go into the room, talk to him in a high-pitched voice, sit, and wait for him to come to you. When your kitten is frightened, his natural instinct is to hide. Let the kitten hide! The worst thing you can do is to pull the kitten out of the hiding place and try to comfort him. You are precisely what he is afraid of, and forcing him to confront you will not help.

Kittens vary in their adjustment to a new home. He may come running right over to you. But if he's shy, he may just poke his head out and view you from a distance. Spend 5 minutes in the room, and then leave again for 10 minutes. Each time you go back, your kitten will be braver.

The way to a kitten's heart is through play! Once your kitten calms down, try to coax him out with a toy, and play with him. Once your kitten consistently comes toward you as soon as you enter, purring, tail up over his back, he has started to bond with you. At this point you can quietly, slowly, introduce other humans to him in the safe room.

You will bond with your new kitten much more quickly through play than through cuddling. After playing, when your kitten is relaxed and tired, cuddling will be most welcome.

Resist the temptation to invite the neighborhood over to see your new pet. Give him time to become comfortable in his new home.

Introducing a Kitten to an Older Cat

We're going to assume that you will follow our recommendations for getting your kitten settled in your home, by restricting the kitten to a single room at first, and by giving him plenty of time to become comfortable.

So this section is really for the older cat who has already been in residence in your home.

Consider for a moment the situation you are creating. Just suppose that you were to wake up one fine morning, suspecting nothing different, when you find that a total stranger has moved into your home. The stranger smells and looks funny. He eats at your table, sleeps in your bed, uses your toilet, and acts as if he belongs there. And he gets lots of attention, perhaps more than you have been getting.

Wouldn't you be upset? This guidance should help him adjust:

• Cats depend largely on smell to determine whether something is safe or familiar. So while you are bonding with the kitten in one room, his smell, sounds, and presence in the home are gradually changing from threatening to routine.

• When you are ready to introduce your cat to the kitten, close the kitten in the carrier (in his safe room), open the room door, and leave the room. Let your other cat(s) explore the room and inspect the kitten. Go back to the room and observe. There will probably be some growling and hissing. This is normal. The kitten is very adaptable, and will do his best to get along. Be sure to give your older cat plenty of love and support.

• Once the initial hissing has passed, allow them to meet face to face. Be patient. You may have to repeat this step multiple times over a several days. Do not leave them together unsupervised until you are certain they have become friends.

Going to the Veterinarian

All of my cats, and kittens, enjoy going to the vet. They get lots of attention, handled by professionals. The cat carriers are always present in the house, and the cats often sleep in them. And occasionally there are treats to be found in the cat carrier, at unexpected times. They have no negative associations with the carriers.

Always transport your kitten in a cat carrier. Do not ever take a chance on trying to carry your animal from the car into the doctor's office in your arms. Many beloved pets have become spooked and disappeared into the neighborhood, never to return.

This first visit is also the time to discuss how old your kitten should be when he or she is neutered. Do remind your vet that Maine Coons mature more slowly than other breeds.

Food & Water

Be sure your kitten has access to clean drinking water at all times. Wash the bowl regularly (daily) to avoid a buildup of micro-organisms in the water. Metal, glass, and glazed porcelain bowls are best. Stay away from plastic food dishes for your cat. Do not use automatic watering devices, as they are not cleaned often enough.

Maine Coons mature slowly. We recommend kitten food, which is more calorie-dense, for at least 18 months, but they can be eating adult food as well during this time.

Kitty Litter

Be sure to keep the kitty litter clean. If you are planning to let your kitten sit on your lap and be cuddled, you probably want his litter to be clean. Modern litters may look dry on top, because wet waste is wicked to the bottom, but when the kitten scratches to cover or dig a hole, there may be nastiness underneath. This will discourage your kitten from using the litter box. Please check the cleanliness of the litter box often.

Kittens are naturally clean, and they leave a cattery litter-trained. If your kitten has litter accidents, please consider the following:

• Is the litter clean? Is it cleaned regularly?

• Does the box have a cover on it? Those can concentrate urine smell to the point that they sting your kitten's eyes. Try removing the cover and see whether the behavior changes.

• Did the kitty litter get moved? Cats remember the location, not the color and size of the litter box. Your new kitten can handle only so much change at a time.

• Did you change to a different kind of litter? If you change to a different brand of the same type of litter, mix a little of the new in with the old, in increasing amounts, to make the changeover gradual. If the litters are quite different (clay vs. corn), provide both litters in separate litter boxes side by side until the transition is made.

• Does the kitten feel safe where the litter is? Is it easily accessible?

• Was there a major change in your kitten's life? New food? Screaming baby visiting? New pet? Work schedule suddenly means you're rarely at home? Strong chemicals (e.g. insecticides) used near the litter box?

• Is one of your other pets terrorizing your kitten when you are not watching?

• Is there a medical condition that could be causing the problem, such as constipation, diarrhea, or a urinary tract infection?

Toys

Purchased toys are optional. Almost everything can be a toy to a kitten: ping pong balls, bulky shoe laces, a sock with a knot in it, washclothes (clean or dirty, dry or wet), a short length of empty paper towel roll, a rolled up piece of paper, the twist-off part of milk bottle caps, empty thread spools. If your kitten chews and swallows the plastic twist-offs from milk bottles, please do not let him play with them. It's not safe for a kitten to ingest plastic.

Avoid any toys that have elastic strings, bells, or parts small enough to swallow. When you buy cat toys, please remove bells and elastic that he can chew. Keep small objects (safety pins,

pins, paper clips, buttons, bobby pins, rubber bands, thread, etc.) away from your kitten at all times.

Please avoid laser light toys until your cat is full-grown. Laser lights do not follow the rules of the cat universe and can be very confusing for a kitten who is learning how the world works.

Please avoid toys with feathers when your kitten is young. The quill can get stuck in his throat.

Our cats love the kitty shelves and hammocks you can install on a window sill. And they love cat trees. But these are not necessary. Your kitten will find his own favorite spots.

Scratching

None of our cats or kittens has ever developed a habit of clawing or scratching furniture or carpeting. The best way to prevent your cat from scratching the furniture is to provide something else that is more fun to scratch.

If yours starts to do this, here are some things to try:

• Provide a cat scratching post. It must be at least as tall as the cat is when the cat is stretched to full height, up on his hind legs. Rub catnip into the post when you first get it. Add new catnip every few weeks if necessary.

• Keep your kitten's nails clipped. Use nail clippers from a pet store that are designed for the job. Be careful not to clip the nails too close, or they will bleed and hurt, and you will have trouble doing it next time. Just remove the very tip, the sharp part of the nail.

• As a last resort, you can have little shields glued to the ends of your cat's front claws. These will prevent all damage to carpeting and upholstery.

Habits

Tickling - Although it is cute when your kitten is very young, do not tickle his stomach to the point that he scratches and bites. When he does this, he is following natural instinct, and he is pretending to kill a small animal. But if he continues to treat hands this way when he gets bigger, he may hurt you or an unsuspecting child. Replace your delicate hand with a stuffed toy or a pair of socks, and let him scratch and kick that instead!

Climbing - Kittens often go through a period of climbing everything in sight, including curtains and drapes and legs. They do this to protect themselves in the wild. You will not be able to teach your kitten not to do this, but he will stop by 6-8 months, when he grows in size and confidence.

Scruffing - When the mother cat carries her babies around by the scruff of the neck, they relax, knowing they are safe and protected. For the rest of his life, your kitten will automatically relax if you scratch the back of his neck or scruff him. So if he is ever injured, frightened, or aggressive, scruff him to alleviate the situation. By scruffing, you can control and calm your cat with one hand without any danger from being bitten or scratched.

Counters, Tables - Don't ever feed your kitten from your dinner table, or you will be pestered every time you sit down for a meal. Don't feed your kitten on the kitchen counter if you don't want him up there! Don't leave cat food out on the counter — its smell will entice him.

The Dread Mister - If you really must teach your kitten not to do something, the best teacher is a plant sprayer/mister with water in it. Try not to let the kitten associate the unpleasant spraying with you. Being sprayed, very lightly, is so unpleasant to a cat that the mere sight of the bottle will soon stop bad behaviors.

Giving Pills

I always teach a customer to play with his kitten's mouth. Why? So that if, at some point in your cat's life, you have to give pills, some of the sensations will be familiar. So while you are cuddling your kitten, scruff him lightly (grab all that loose skin around his shoulders with your left hand) and hold him upside down (his feet up) on your lap. With your right hand, play with his mouth. Use your finger to open his mouth, touch his tongue, touch his teeth. Be playful, but make this a routine part of your cuddling sessions.

I am a no-nonsense pill giver. Goes down on the first try, without fail, into Maine Coons from 2 to 25 pounds, without injury to either party. Scruff the cat upside down (as described in the previous paragraph). (It's easier if you've made this a routine.) Hold the pill between your thumb and index finger of the other hand. Use the middle finger of that hand to pry the mouth open, and drop the pill into the back of the cat's mouth. Gravity is working in your favor. Land it at the very back of the mouth, and the cat will never taste it but will instinctively swallow it. If necessary, you can push it down a bit with your finger.

Summary

If, as you embark on this new adventure with a Maine Coon kitten, you give your kitten plenty of time to adjust to you and to his new "forever home," he will be prepared to give you years of love, attention, entertainment, and companionship. Your new Maine Coon will become one of the joys of your life.

Robin Warren - Red Flannel Cattery

http://redflannelcattery.com

Relevant Websites

The Cat Fancier's Association
http://www.cfa.org/Breeds/BreedsKthruR/MaineCoon.aspx

The International Cat Association
http://www.tica.org/public/breeds/mc/intro.php?zoom_highlight=maine+coon

United Maine Coon Cat Association
http://www.cffinc.org/umcca/main.htm

Maine Coon Rescue
http://www.mainecoonrescue.net/

East Coast Maine Coon Rescue
http://www.ecmcr.org/

The Governing Council of the Cat Fancy
http://www.gccfcats.org/

Maine Coon Breed Society
http://www.mainecoonbreedsociety.com/

The Maine Coon Cat Club
http://www.maine-coon-cat-club.com/

Glossary

A

Ailurophile - A lover of cats.

Ailurophobe - One who fears and/or hates cats.

Allergen - The primary allergen produced by cats to which sensitive individuals react is the protein Fel d 1 produced by the animal's sebaceous and salivary glands. Fel d 1 is especially spread in the environment by dried flakes of saliva on the fur from grooming.

Allergy - An individual exhibiting a high degree of sensitivity to a known irritant, as in the Fel d 1 in cats. The symptoms of the allergic reaction may include sneezing, itching, and watering of the eyes, and skin rashes.

Alter - A term used in reference to the surgical procedures that render companion animals incapable of reproduction i.e. neutering or spaying.

B

Bloodline - A bloodline establishes an animal's pedigree by supplying a verifiable line of descent. Catteries carefully cultivate their animals' bloodlines in an effort to produce the highest possible exemplars of the given breed.

Breed Standard - Breed clubs and official feline organizations like The International Cat Association (TICA) formulate standards of excellence for breed to be used as a basis for evaluation the quality of the animals for breeding and showing purposes.

Breed - An animal is said to belong to a particular breed when it shares specifically defined physical characteristics derived from a common ancestry that "breed true" or are reliable passed on to subsequent generations.

Breeder - A breeder is an individual who works to produce superior examples of a given breed of cat (or other animal) through the carefully selected pairing of dams and sires. The principle purpose of breeding is to both maintain and improve the genetic quality of the breed in question.

Breeding - Breeding refers to the pairing of dams and sires in controlled reproductive programs for the express purpose of producing high quality offspring.

Breeding Program - A breeding program is a planned mating of carefully chosen dams and sires to cultivate ideal examples of a given breed.

Breeding Quality - An animal's breed quality describes the degree to which an individual conforms to the breed standard for subsequent purposes of show or participation in a breeding program.

Breed True - When male and female cats of a given breed mate and produce offspring that possess the same traits, all conforming to the recognized standard for the breed, the line is said to "breed true."

C

Carpal Pads - A cat's carpal pads are located on the front legs at the region roughly correlating with the human wrist. Their purpose is to provide greater traction for the animal while walking.

Castrate - The surgical removal of a male cat's testicles to render him incapable of impregnating females.

Caterwaul - A shrill and discordant feline vocalization.

Cat Fancy - The "cat fancy" is an aggregate term to define all of the groups, associations, and clubs as well as their members that exist for the purpose of breeding and showing cats.

Catnip - Cat nip (Nepeta cataria) is a perennial herb containing high levels of an aromatic oil to which cats are strongly attracted. In response to exposure to "nip," cats display a kind of intoxication similar to what humans experience when they are "stoned." A cat must be older than 8-9 months of age to respond to catnip, and some individuals are completely immune to the herb's effects.

Cattery - A cattery is a facility where cats are kept for the purpose of breeding to promulgate a specific breed and bloodline.

Certified Pedigree - A certified pedigree is one that has been officially issued by a feline registering association.

Clowder - The collective term "clowder" refers to an assemblage or group of cats.

Coat - The overall term used in reference to a cat's fur.

Crate - A crate is a container used for the safe transport or temporary confinement of cats and other small companion animals.

Crepuscular - The correct term to describe the times at which cats are most active, dawn and dusk. Contrary to popular perception, cats are not nocturnal.

Crossbred - When a dam and sire of different breeds produce offspring, the kittens are said to be crossbred.

D

Dam - In a breeding pair of cats, the female is the dam. Also called a queen.

Dander - Dander is often responsible for the allergic reaction some sensitive people display in the presence of cats. The small scales are shed by the animal's hair and skin, and contain the Fel d 1 protein from the animal's saliva transferred during self-grooming.

Declawing - Declawing is a surgical procedure to amputate the last digit of a cat's feet for the purpose of removing its claws. The operation is illegal in Europe, and also in many parts of the United States. Declawing is highly controversial and generally considered to be inhumane and cruel.

Desex - Desexing is the alteration of an animal by neutering or spaying to render the individual incapable of reproduction.

Domesticated - Animals that live and/or work tamely with humans whether by training or choice.

E

Ear Mites - Ear mites are microscopic parasites that cause extreme itching and discomfort by feeding on the lining of a cat's ear canal. Their presence generates a strong, foul odor and causes a build-up of black, tarry debris.

Entire - A cat is said to be "entire" when the individual is in possession of its complete reproductive system.

Exhibitor - An individual who participates in an organized cat show competitively with his or her animal or animals.

F

Fel d 1 - The Fel d 1 protein is produced by a cat's sebaceous glands and is also present in the animal's saliva. This is the substance that triggers an adverse allergic reaction in some sensitive people.

Feline - Felines are members of the family *Felidae*, which includes lions, tigers, jaguars, and both wild and domestic cats.

Fleas - Fleas are wingless, bloodsucking insects in the order *Siphonaptera* that feed off warm-blooded animals causing scratching and skin irritation, and in severe cases, anemia.

Flehmening/Flehmen Reaction - The Flehmen Reaction is a facial gesture in cats often mistaken for a grimace. When a cat partially opens its mouth and curls back its upper lip, the animal is drawing air over two special openings in the roof of the mouth just behind the front teeth. These second "nostrils" allow a cat to "taste" what it is smelling.

G

Gene pool - In any population of organisms, the "gene pool" is the group's collective genetic information.

Genes - Genes are the distinct hereditary units consisting of a DNA sequence that occupies a specific location on a chromosome. Genes determine the particular physical characteristics of an organism.

Genetic - Any trait, characteristic, tendency, or condition that is inherited is said to be genetic in nature.

Genetically Linked Defects - Specific health conditions or other perceived flaws that are passed from one generation to the next are considered to be genetically linked defects.

Genetics - Genetics is the scientific study of heredity.

Genotype - The genetic makeup of an organism or a group of organisms is called the genotype.

Grooming - The necessary procedures to care for the coat of a feline are called grooming and typically include brushing, combing, trimming, or washing.

H

Heat - When a female mammal such as a cat enters her seasonal estrus cycle the phase is colloquially referred to as "going into heat."

Hereditary - Characteristics, traits, diseases, or conditions genetically transmitted from parent to offspring are said to be hereditary.

Histamine - A physiologically active amine released by mast cells in plant and animal tissue as part of an allergic reaction.

Hock - The anatomical term for that part of a cat's hind leg that is the rough equivalent of the human ankle.

Housetraining - The process of teaching an animal to live cleanly in a house using a box of sand or gavel litter for urination and defecation is called "housebreaking."

I

Immunization - Immunizations, also called inoculations or vaccinations, are injections intended to create immunity against disease.

Innate - Qualities, traits, and tendencies that are present at birth and therefore inborn are said to be innate.

Inbreeding - The mating of two closely-related cats is said to be inbreeding, and is typically the cause of genetic defects.

Instinct - Inborn patterns of behavior in a species that are triggered by specific environmental stimuli are called "instincts."

Intact - Intact animals have not been spayed or neutered and are in possession of their complete reproductive system.

J

Jacobsen's Organ - This is a highly specialized organ in the roof of a cat's mouth. Two extra "nostrils" located just behind the upper front teeth allow the cat to "taste" a scent when air passes over the openings.

K

Kindle - A "kindle" is a collective term for a group of cats, but in this instance refers specifically to kittens.

Kitten - A kitten is a cat of less than 6 months of age.

L

Lactation - The formation and secretion of milk by the mammary glands for the nourishment of young mammals.

Litter - Felines give birth to 3-4 kittens on average, with 6-10 possible. These multiple offspring groups are referred to as litters.

Litter Box - A litter box is a container holding sand or clay that allows a cat to live cleanly in the house by providing the animal with an acceptable place to urinate and defecate.

Longhaired - Any breed of cats, like a Persian, that have a coat made up of varying lengths of long hair. These same animals usually also display prominent neck ruffs and plumed tails.

M

Mites - Tiny parasites from the order *Acarina* are called mites. They infest both plants and animals, and are often present in the ear canals of domestic cats.

Muzzle - That part of the head and face of a cat that projects forward. This region includes the mouth, nose, and jaws, and may also be referred to as the snout.

N

Neuter - A term used to describe the surgery for castrating a male cat to prevent him from impregnating a female.

Nictitating Membrane - The nictitating membrane is the transparent inner or "third" eyelid on cats that protects and moistens the eye.

Nocturnal - Animals that are nocturnal are most active at night. This term is used in error with cats as these creatures are most active at dusk and dawn and are therefore crepuscular.

O

Odd-Eyed - In odd-eyed cats, each eye is a different color.

P

Papers - The colloquial term for the official documentation of a cat's pedigree and registration is "papers."

Pedigree - A pedigree is the written verifiable ancestry of a cat of a particular breed spanning three or more generations.

Pet Quality - A pet quality pedigreed cat is one that fails to sufficiently conform to the standard for the breed to be used in a breeding program or to be exhibited for competition.

Q

Queen - Queens are intact female cats in possession of their complete reproductive system.

Quick - The "quick" of a cat's claw is the vascular portion at the base that will bleed profusely if accidentally clipped.

R

Rabies - Rabies is a highly infectious viral disease fatal in warm-blooded animals. It is transmitted by the bite of an infected animal and attacks the victim's central nervous system.

Registered Cat - A registered cat is one that has been

documented via a recognized feline association in regard to its breed and pedigree.

Registered Name - A cat's registered name is the name used to verify its breed and pedigree. Names are typically long, and made up of a combination of the names of the cat's sire and dam.

S

Scratching Post - Any structure covered in carpet or rope and designed to be used by a cat to sharpen and clean its claws without being destructive to household furnishings is referred to as a scratching "post."

Show - Cat shows are organized exhibition where cats are judged competitively for the degree to which they conform to accepted breed standards.

Show Quality - Show quality cats in any breed are those that conform sufficiently to the recognized standard for their type to be included in breeding programs and to be exhibited in competitions.

Sire - In a breeding pair of cats, the male is referred to as the sire.

Spay - Spaying is the surgical procedure whereby a female cat's ovaries are removed rendering her incapable of reproduction.

Spray - Spraying is a territorial behavior typically seen in male cats. Using a stream of pungent urine, the cat marks its territory, often as part of a competition with other males for the attention of a female.

Stud - Studs are male cats that are intact and are therefore qualified to participate in a breeding program.

Subcutaneous - Subcutaneous means just below the skin, and typically refers to an injection or to the administration of supplemental fluids in cats with kidney deficiencies.

T

Tapetum Lucidum - The tapetum lucidum is the interior portion of a cat's eye. The structure is highly reflective and helps the cat to see effectively in low light. Cats cannot, however, see in total darkness.

V

Vaccine - Vaccines are dead or weakened preparations of a bacterium, virus, or other pathogen. They are injected into an individual for the purpose of stimulating the production of antibodies to cultivate immunity against disease.

W

Wean - Weaning is the point in a kitten's development when it gradually gives up its mother's milk as its primary means of nutrition and begins to take solid foods.

Whisker Break - The whisker break on a cat is an indentation on the upper jaw.

Whisker Pad - The thickened or fatty pads on either side of a cat's face holding rows of sensory whiskers.

Whole - A cat of either gender that is in possession of its reproductive system is said to be whole.

Index

Lightning Source UK Ltd.
Milton Keynes UK
UKHW021329010920
369163UK00011B/2244

9 780992 784355